The Incas of Peru
By Clements Markham

PREFACE

THE fascinating story of Inca civilisation was told to our fathers by Dr. Robertson, whose 'History of America' appeared in 1778, and to ourselves by Mr. Prescott, whose 'Conquest of Peru' was published in 1843. It is assumed that most educated people have read the latter work. But since its publication a great deal of subsequently discovered material has quite altered our view of some things, and thrown entirely new light upon others. Yet Mr. Prescott's work can never lose its high position as a carefully written and very charming history.

It is now more than sixty years ago since the present writer came under the influence of that fascination, when, as a naval cadet on board H.M.S. *Collingwood*, the flagship in the Pacific, he first gazed on the land of the Incas. The noble Symondite line-of-battle ship rounded the northern headland of San Lorenzo Island, and made her stately way to her anchorage in Callao roads. I was just fourteen, and under the wing of Lieutenant Peel, aged nineteen (afterwards the gallant Sir William Peel), who was officer of my watch on the forecastle. We gazed on the scene before us, the bright green plain rising by a gentle slope to the mountains, with the white towers of Lima appearing on its further skirts, and behind the mighty cordillera rising into the clouds. During the four years of our commission we were five times at Callao, staying some months at a time. I got to know Lima very well, and made some friends, including the beautiful Grimanesa Althaus, to whom I was afterwards much indebted in my researches; and the aged Señora O'Higgins, daughter of the Spanish Viceroy of Peru from 1796 to 1801. I knew the banks of the Eimac between Lima and its mouth even better, and I visited the vast mounds or *huacas* in the plain. In those days youngsters on the Pacific station were carefully taught French and Spanish, as well as navigation.

It was not until my return, in 1848, that I was able to obtain a copy of Prescott's 'Conquest of Peru,' which I devoured over and over again with intense interest. During the winter of my service in the Arctic regions I had a copy of the Quichua Dictionary by Torres Rubio to study, which I had bought in Lima, and the Doctor had Holguin's grammar, so that I was able to acquire some knowledge of the language of the Incas. On my return I studied all the authorities within my reach, and in August 1852 I resolved to undertake an expedition to Peru. I was practised in observing the heavenly bodies for latitude and longitude, and I could make a fairly good survey of ruins, and maps of my routes.

My first care was to obtain Mr. Prescott's approval of my undertaking, and I went to Boston with introductions to him from Lord Carlisle and the Dean of St. Paul's (Milman). He at once invited me to his country house at Pepperell, in New Hampshire, where I enjoyed his society for ten very pleasant days. Our party consisted of Mr. and Mrs. Prescott, their son Amory, the secretary and myself. Mr. Prescott's house was a long wooden building with a covered verandah extending half its length, tall shady trees in front, on a lawn dividing the house from a quiet country road. There was a pleasant shady walk behind the house, of which Mr. Prescott was very fond; for, though his sight was bad, he was not quite blind. He could see enough to get about the house, and even to take walks by himself, but not to read.

He conversed with me in his large study, where he took notes on a slate with lines, while his secretary read to him. The notes were then read to him, and, after some thought, he began to dictate. We talked over Peru, and he explained most lucidly the comparative value of the authorities he had used, adding that there were probably others of equal importance that he had not seen. Once he said that no history could be quite satisfactory unless the author was personally acquainted with the localities he had to describe.

He gave me valuable advice, and said that he would be much interested in the results of my journey. I used to drive over the country in a buggy, and pull on the quiet little Nississisett river with Amory. My stay of ten days at Pepperell, with the great historian, is a time which I always look back to with feelings of pleasure and gratitude. It was a fitting introduction to my Peruvian researches.

From Lima I made several excursions, and explored the coast from Lima to Nasca. Crossing an unfrequented pass of the Andes from Yca, I made several excursions from my headquarters at Ayacucho, and eventually went thence to Cuzco. At the city of the Incas I remained several weeks, carefully examining the ruins, and learning much from such recipients of folklore as Dr. Julian Ochoa and the Señora Astete. From Cuzco I went to the valley of Vilcamayu occupied in researches, and then over the Andes to spend a fortnight with Dr. Justiniani, a descendant of the Incas, at Laris, and to copy his manuscripts. My next journey was to Paucartambo, whence I penetrated far into the wild montaña. Finally I went from Cuzco to Arequipa by the lofty pass of Rumihuasi.

On my return to England I continued my studies until, in 1859 to 1861, I was engaged on the important public service of introducing the cultivation of the various species of quinine-yielding chinchona trees from South America into British India. I had the pleasure of making the acquaintance of that splendid old warrior, General Miller, who referred me to new mines of information among the '*Papeles Varios*' of the Lima library. During my journeys I was able to explore great part of the northern half of the basin of Lake Titicaca, and the Montaña of Caravaya. I also collected several Quichua songs. Throughout my journeys in Peru I received the heartiest welcomes and the most unbounded hospitality and kindness. The three Indians who went with me into the forests of Caravaya were obliging, willing, and faithful. My experience with them and others gave me a high opinion of the Indian character.

Since my return from Peru, nearly fifty years ago, I have kept up my knowledge of the literary labours of the Peruvians, in the direction of Inca research, by correspondence with friends, and the receipt of books and pamphlets. My most valued correspondents have been Don E. Larrabure y Unanue, Don Manuel Gonzalez de la Rosa, Don José Toribio Polo, and Don Ricardo Palma. I also received much kind assistance from friends in Spain, now departed, Don Pascual de

Gayangos, and especially from Don Marcos Jimenez de la Espada. The literary labours of these and other Spanish and Peruvian authors attain a high standard. I have since devoted my efforts to a complete mastery of all the original authorities on Inca history and civilisation. It is not enough to dip into them, nor even to read them, in order to obtain such a mastery. The problems that present themselves in the study of Inca civilisation are often complicated, they need much weighing of evidence, and are difficult of solution. My own studies have extended over many years, during which time I have translated and annotated the principal authorities, made indexes, and compared their various statements on each point as it arises. Without such thoroughness, an author is scarcely justified in entering upon so difficult and complicated an inquiry.

Having reached my eightieth birthday, I have abandoned the idea of completing a detailed history which I once entertained. But I have felt that a series of essays, based upon my researches, might at all events be published with advantage, as the subject is one of general interest, alike fascinating and historically important, and as the results of the studies of a lifetime are likely to be of some value. In the form in which the essays are presented, it is my hope that they will be interesting to the general reader, while offering useful material for study to the more serious historical student.

I have added, as appendices, a translation of the Inca drama of Ollantay; and a curious love story told to Morua by Amautas, in about 1585. It is one of the very few remains of ancient Inca folklore.

The accompanying map is used for the illustration of this work by permission of the council of the Royal Geographical Society. The original compilation and drawing has been made on a scale of 1: 1,000,000 in four sheets; but for the purpose of publication the map has been reduced to a scale of 1: 2,000,000. The map extends from 8 to 18 S. and from 65 to 74 W., the area included being about 418,000 square miles. No regular surveys exist of the region as a whole, nor are any likely to be undertaken for years to come. Consequently, for the greater part of it, the mapping has depended upon route traverses varying considerably in merit, but fairly good in cases where astronomical observations have been taken.

The compilation and drawing has taken two years, and has necessitated comparing and determining the value of a large amount of cartographical material and many observations.

About sixty observed positions for latitude and twenty for longitude have been accepted, and the materials used include thirty-two recent maps and reports. The map includes the original land of the Incas, the basin of Lake Titicaca, and the eastern montaña.

I have to thank the Government of Peru and the Lima Geographical Society, as well as many others, for much valuable assistance in the provision of materials. The very difficult work of compilation has been admirably done by Mr. Reeves, the accomplished Map Curator of the Royal Geographical Society, and by Mr. Batchelor, the very able draughtsman.

CLEMENTS R. MARKHAM.

21 ECCLESTON SQUARE, S.W,
      July 1910

THE INCAS OF PERU

CHAPTER I. THE TELLERS OF THE STORY

BEFORE entering upon a contemplation of the Inca history and civilisation, a story of no ordinary interest, it seems natural to wish for some acquaintance with those who told the story. It is not intended to enter upon a full critical examination of their work. That has been done elsewhere. It will suffice to give a more popular account of the tellers of the story.

Rude and destructive as most of the Spanish conquerors were, and as all are generally supposed to have been, there were some who sympathised with the conquered people, were filled with admiration at their civilisation and the excellent results of their rule, and were capable of making researches and recording their impressions. Nor were these authors confined to the learned professions. First and foremost were the military writers. Some of their works are lost to us, but the narratives of at least four have been preserved.

Among these Pedro de Cieza de Leon takes the first and most honourable place. Imagine a little boy of fourteen entering upon a soldier's life in the undiscovered wilds of South America, and, without further instruction, becoming the highest authority on Inca history. It seems wonderful, yet it was at the early age of fourteen that Cieza de Leon embarked for the new world. He was born in 1519 at the town of Llerena, in Estremadura, about nineteen leagues east of Badajos, at the foot of the Sierra de San Miguel, a Moorish looking place surrounded by a wall with brick towers, and five great gates. It produced several distinguished men, including Juan de Pozo, the watchmaker who placed the *giralda* on the tower of Seville Cathedral. At Llerena Pedro de Cieza passed his childhood, but his boyhood was scarce begun when he embarked at Seville; serving under Pedro de Heredia, the founder and first governor of Carthagena, on the Spanish Main. Soon afterwards, in

1538, young Pedro de Cieza joined the expedition of Vadillo up the valley of the Cauca. At an age when most boys are at school, this lad had been sharing all the hardships and perils of seasoned veterans, and even then he was gifted with powers of observation far beyond his years.

The character of our soldier chronicler was destined to be formed in a rough and savage school. It is certainly most remarkable that so fine a character should have been formed amidst all the horrors of the Spanish American conquests. Humane, generous, full of noble sympathies, observant and methodical; he was bred amidst scenes of cruelty, pillage, and wanton destruction, which were calculated to produce a far different character. Considering the circumstances in which he was placed from early boyhood, his book is certainly a most extraordinary, as well as a most valuable, result of his military services and researches. He began to write a journal when serving under Robledo in the Cauca valley in 1541. He says: 'As I noted the many great and strange things that are to be seen in the new world of the Indies there came upon me a strong desire to write an account of some of them, as well those which I have seen with my own eyes as those I heard of from persons of good repute.' In another place he says: 'Oftentimes when the other soldiers were sleeping, I was tiring myself in writing. Neither fatigue nor the ruggedness of the country, nor the mountains and rivers, nor intolerable hunger and suffering, have ever been sufficient to obstruct my two duties, namely, writing and following my flag and my captain without fault.'

Cieza de Leon made his way by land to Quito, and then travelled all over Peru collecting information. He finished the first part of his 'Chronicle' in September 1550, when at the age of thirty-two. It is mainly a geographical description of the country, with sailing directions for the coast, and an account of the Inca roads and bridges. In the second part he reviewed the system of government of the Incas, with the events of each reign. He spared no pains to obtain the best and most authentic information, and in 1550 he went to Cuzco to confer with one of the surviving Incas. His sympathy with the conquered people, and generous appreciation of their many good qualities, give a special charm to his narrative.

Cieza de Leon stands first in the first rank of authorities on Inca civilisation.

Another soldier-author was Juan de Betanzos. We first hear of his book from Friar Gregorio de Garcia, who wrote his 'Origen de los Indios' in 1607. He announced that he possessed the manuscript of Betanzos, and he made great use of it, copying the first two chapters wholesale. The incomplete manuscript in the Escurial, of which Prescott had a copy, only contains the eighteen first chapters and part of another. It was edited and printed in 1880 by Jimenez de la Espada. The complete manuscript which belonged to Garcia has not been found. Juan de Betanzos was probably from Galicia, and came to Peru with Hernando Pizarro. He became a citizen of Cuzco, and married a daughter of the Inca Atahualpa. Betanzos took great pains to learn the Quichua language, and was employed to negotiate with the Incas in Vilcapampa. He was appointed official interpreter to the Audiencia and to successive Viceroys. His principal work, entitled 'Suma y narracion de los Incas,' was composed by order of the Viceroy, Don Antonio de Mendoza, and was finished in 1551, but was not published owing to the Viceroy's death. He also wrote a 'Doctrina,' and two vocabularies which are lost. The date of the death of Betanzos is unknown, but he certainly lived twenty years after he wrote the 'Suma y narracion.' Betanzos was imbued with the spirit of the natives, and he has portrayed native feeling and character as no other Spaniard could have done. He gives an excellent and almost dramatic account of the Chanca war with the Incas, and his versions of the early myths are important. He ranks next to Cieza de Leon as an authority.

Sarmiento, a militant sailor, is the highest authority as regards the historical events of the Inca period, though his work has only quite recently been brought to light. The beautiful manuscript, illustrated with coats of arms, found its way into the library of Gronovius, and was bought for the University of Gottingen in 1785. It remained in the university library, unnoticed, for 120 years. But, in August 1906, the learned librarian, Dr. Pietschmann, published the text at Berlin, carefully edited and annotated and with a valuable introduction.

Pedro Sarmiento de Gamboa was a seaman of some distinction, and was a leader in Mandana's voyage to the Solomon Islands. He accompanied the Viceroy Toledo, and was employed by that statesman to write a history of the Incas. It is without doubt the most authentic and reliable we possess, as regards the course of events. For it was compiled from the carefully attested evidence of the Incas themselves, who were officially examined on oath, so that Sarmiento had the means of obtaining accurate information which no other writer possessed. The chapters were afterwards read over to the forty-two Incas who gave evidence, in their own language, and received their final corrections. The history was finished and sent to Spain in 1572.

Pedro Pizarro, who was a cousin of the conqueror, went to Peru as his page when only fifteen. He eventually retired to Arequipa, where he wrote his 'Relaciones,' finished in 1571. Prescott had a copy of the manuscript, but it was not printed until quite recently. There were other writers among the military men, notably Francisco de Chaves, but their work is lost to us.

Among the lawyers the work of Zarate was published in 1555, differing a good deal from the manuscript, and it is not of much value. The writings of the licentiate Polo de Ondegardo are more important. He occupied the post of Corregidor of Cuzco in 1560, and accompanied the Viceroy Toledo on his journey of inspection ten years afterwards. He made researches into the laws and administration of the Incas, but his knowledge of the language was limited. His two 'Relaciones' were written in 1561 and 1570. They have never been printed. Prescott had copies of them. Another 'Report' by Polo is in the National Library at Madrid. It describes the division and tenure of land, and some administrative details. The 'Relacion' of Fernando de Santillan is of about the same value, and was written at the same period. It is mainly devoted to a discussion of the laws and customs relating to the collection of tribute. The licentiate Juan de Matienza was a contemporary of Ondegardo and Santillan, and discussed the ancient institutions with the same objects. His manuscript is in the British Museum. In the following century Juan de Solorzano digested the numerous laws in the 'Politica Indiana,' and the prolific legislation of the Viceroy Toledo is embodied in the 'Ordenanzas del Peru,' published at Lima in 1683. All the lawyers who studied the subject express their admiration of the government of the Incas.

The geographers were the local officials who were ordered to draw up topographical reports on their several provinces. Most of these reports were written between 1570 and 1590, and they naturally vary very much in value. The 'Relaciones Geograficas de Indias (Peru)' were published at Madrid in four large volumes, between 1881 and 1897.

The priests were the most diligent inquirers respecting the native religion, rites and ceremonies. The first priest who came with Pizarro was the Dominican friar, Vicente de Valverde. He wrote a 'Carta Relacion' on the affairs of Peru, and some letters to Charles V, containing original information, but he left the country in 1541, and was there too short a time for his writings to be of much value. The best known clerical author on Peru was the Jesuit Josef de Acosta, who was born at Medina del Campo in 1540, and was in Peru from 1570 to 1586, travelling over all parts of the country. He then went to Mexico, and died at Salamanca in 1600. His great work, 'Historia Natural de las Indias,' in its complete form, was first published at Seville in 1590. Hakluyt and Purchas gave extracts from it, and the whole work was translated into English in 1604 by Edward Grimston. It was much used by subsequent writers. The Inca Garcilasso quotes it twenty-seven times, and Prescott nineteen times. Acosta's work will always be valuable, but he was superficial and an indifferent Quichua scholar. He is superseded in several branches of his subject by writers whose works have become known in recent years.

Among these the most important is Cristoval de Molina, priest of the hospital for natives at Cuzco, who wrote a 'Report on the Fables and Rites of the Incas' addressed to the Bishop Artaun, 1570-84. Molina had peculiar opportunities for collecting accurate information. He was a master of the Quichua language, he examined native chiefs and learned men who could remember the Inca Empire in the days of its prosperity, and his position at the hospital at Cuzco gave him an intimate acquaintance with the native character. Molina gives very interesting accounts of the periodical festivals and the religion, and twelve prayers in the original Quichua. Very intimately connected with the work of Molina is that of Miguel Cavello Balboa, who wrote at Quito between 1576 and 1586. In the opening address of Molina to the Bishop he mentions a previous account which he had submitted on the origin, history, and government of the Incas. This account appears to have been procured and appropriated by Balboa, who tells us that his history is based on the learned writings of Cristoval de Molina.

Miguel Cavello Balboa was a soldier who took orders late in life and went out to Peru in 1566. He settled at Quito and devoted himself to the preparation of his work entitled 'Miscellanea Austral.' He is the only authority who gives any tradition respecting the origin of the coast people; and he supplies an excellent narrative of the war between Huascar and Atahualpa, including the love episode of Quilacu.

The history of the Incas by Friar Martin de Morua is still in manuscript. Morua had studied the Quichua language. His work, finished in 1590, is full of valuable information. A copy of the manuscript was obtained by Dr. Gonzalez de la Rosa from the Loyola archives in 1909.

Some of the Jesuits were engaged in the work of extirpating idolatry. Their reports throw light on the legends and superstitions of the people on and near the coast. These are contained in the very rare work of Arriaga (1621), and in the report of Avila on the legends and myths of Huarochiri. The work of another Jesuit named Luis de Teruel, who wrote an account of his labours for the extirpation of idolatry, is lost, as well as that of Hernando Avendaño, some of whose sermons in Quichua have been preserved. Fray Alonzo Ramos Gavilan, in his 'History of the Church of Copacabana' (1620), throws light on the movements of the *mitimaes* or colonists in the Collao, and gives some new details respecting the consecrated virgins, the sacrifices, and the deities worshipped on the shores of lake Titicaca. The 'Coronica Moralizada,' by Antonio de la Calancha (1638-53), is a voluminous record of the Order of St. Augustine in Peru. There is a good deal that is interesting and important scattered among the stories of martyrdoms and miracles of the Augustine friars. Calancha gives many details respecting the manners and customs of the Indians, and the topography of the country. He is the only writer who has given any .account of the religion of the Chimu. He also gives the most accurate version of the Inca calendar. The chronicle of the Franciscans by Diego de Cordova y Salinas, published at Madrid in 1643, is of less value.

Fernando Montesinos, born at Cuenca, was in holy orders and a licentiate in canon law. He appears to have gone to Peru in 1629, in the train of the Viceroy Count of Chinchon. After filling some appointments, he gave himself up entirely to historical researches and mining speculations, travelling over all parts of Peru. In 1639 he came to live at Lima, and he was employed to write an account of the 'Auto de Fé' in that year. He also published a book on the workings of metals. The last date which shows Montesinos to have been in Peru is 1642. After his return to Spain he became cura of a village near Seville, and in 1644 he submitted a memorial to the King asking for some dignity as a reward for his services.

Montesinos wrote 'Ophir de España, Memorias Historiales y Politicas del Peru.' The long list of Kings of Peru given by Montesinos did not originate with him, but was due to earlier writers long before his time. He, however, collected some interesting traditions, but his absurd contention that Peru was peopled by Armenians under the leadership of Noah's great-grandson Ophir destroys all confidence in his statements.

The work of Montesinos was found by Muñoz in the convent of San José at Seville. Muñoz got possession of the manuscripts, and Ternauax Compans obtained a copy, of which he published a French translation in 1840. The manuscripts were brought to Madrid, and Jimenez de la Espada published the second book, containing the long list of Peruvian Kings, in 1882.

By far the greatest of the clerical authors who wrote on Inca civilisation had the advantage of being a mestizo. Blas Valera was the son of Lius de Valera, a soldier of the conquest, by a Peruvian lady of the court of Atahualpa, and was born at Chachapoyas in about 1540. He was brought up at Caxamarca, and afterwards at Truxillo, until his twentieth year. At Truxillo he learnt Latin, while Quichua was his native tongue. He took orders at the age of twenty-eight, and became a Jesuit. In 1571 he was sent to Cuzco as a catechist, and was there for at least ten years. He then went to Juli and La Paz, and later was at Quito and in the northern parts of Peru. In about 1594 he embarked at Callao for Cadiz. He was in that city when it was taken by the English under the Earl of Essex in 1596. But the Jesuits were allowed to depart with their papers. Blas Valera died soon afterwards.

Blas Valera had qualifications and advantages possessed by no other writer. The Inca Garcilasso knew Quichua, but he was a child, and only twenty when he went to Spain. It was after an interval of forty years that he thought of writing about his native country. Blas Valera, like Garcilasso, was half a Peruvian, and Quichua was his native language. But unlike Garcilasso, instead of going to Spain when he was twenty, he worked for Peru and its people for thirty years, devoting himself to a study of the history, literature, and ancient customs of his countrymen, receiving their records and legends from the older Amautas and *Quipucamayocs* who could remember the Inca rule, and their lists of kings. His perfect mastery of the language enabled him to do this with a thoroughness which no Spaniard could approach.

Blas Valera brought his writings with him to Spain, doubtless with a view to publication. He had written a 'Historia del Peru' in Latin which, after his death, was given to the Inca Garcilasso, who made very extensive use of it. According to the bibliographers, Antonio and Leon Pinelo, another work by Blas Valera was 'De los Indies del Peru, sus costumbres y pacificacion.' It was lost. But in 1879 Jimenez de la Espada found a most valuable manuscript on the same subject without the name of the author. He published it under the name of the 'Anonymous Jesuit.' Dr. Gonzalez de la Rosa has brought forward arguments, which appear to be quite conclusive, and which are given in another place, that the anonymous Jesuit was no other than Blas Valera. Another work of the learned mestizo, also lost, was entitled 'Vocabulario Historico del Peru.' It was brought from Cadiz to the college of La Paz in 1604, by the Procurador of the Jesuits, named Diego Torres Vasquez. It was this work that contained the long lists of kings. This is clear from the statement of Father Anello Oliva in his history of distinguished men of the Company of Jesus, written in 1631. Oliva had seen the 'Vocabulario Historico del Peru,' and learnt from it the great antiquity of the Peruvian kingdom. Montesinos no doubt copied his list from the 'Vocabulario,' which was then at La Paz. The premature death of Blas Valera, and the disposal of his valuable manuscripts, is the most deplorable loss that the history of Inca civilisation has sustained.

The work of a more recent author has come to light through the diligence of Jimenez de la Espada. This is the history of the New World by Father Bernabe Cobos, in four large volumes. It is a valuable addition to our authorities on ancient Peru, and is more especially valuable for its chapters containing full accounts of the minerals, medicinal plants and edible vegetables, and of the fauna of Peru.

A narrative has been recently brought to light by Don Carlos Romero, in the *Revista Historica*, of Lima, written by a Dominican monk named Reginaldo de Lizarraga, in about 1605. It is entitled 'Descripcion de las Indias,' and consists of two parts, one geographical and the other chiefly biographical. Lizarraga travelled all over the country, from Quito to the most southern part of Chile. Finally, he became Bishop of Asuncion in Paraguay, where he died in about 1612.

The geographical descriptions of Lizarraga are sketchy and unequal to those of Cieza de Leon, and he is very unsympathetic when referring to the Incas, or to the unfortunate Indians. His work is mainly occupied with brief notices of prelates and viceroys, devoting more space to the proceedings of the Viceroy Toledo. There are only two statements of interest in his work. One is that a wall was built on the pass of Vilcañota, to divide the territory of the Incas from that of the Collas. In another he gives what is clearly the correct story about Mancio Serra de Leguisamo having gambled away the great image of the sun in one night. These statements will be referred to in their places.

Blas Valera and the Inca Garcilasso are the two mestizo authors. The latter is so important a personage that a separate essay is devoted to his biography.

Gomara and Herrera were never in the country, and writers living after the end of the seventeenth century have no claim to be looked upon as original authorities.

There were two pure-blooded Indians whose writings are of very great value. The first was a chief living near the borders of Collahua, south of Cuzco, calling himself Juan de Santa Cruz Pachacuti Yamqui Salcamayhua, who wrote his account of the antiquities of Peru in about 1620. I found the manuscript in the National Library at Madrid, and the Hakluyt Society published my translation in 1873. The Spanish text was afterwards edited and published by Jimenez de la Espada. It gives the traditions of the Incas, as they were handed down by the grandchildren of those who were living at the time of the Spanish conquest to *their* grandchildren. They are entitled to a certain authority, and Salcamayhua gives three Quichua prayers to the Supreme Being which are of extraordinary interest.

The work of the second Indian author is quite a recent discovery. It was found by Dr. Pietschmann, the librarian of the University of Göttingen, in the Royal Library at Copenhagen in 1908. The title is 'Nueva Coronica y Buen Gobierno,' de Don Felipe Huaman Poma de Ayala; a very thick quarto of 1179 pages, with numerous clever pen-

and-ink sketches, almost one for every page. There is a particular account of the author's ancestry, for not only did he descend from Yarrovilca, Lord of Huanuco, but his mother was a daughter of the great Inca Tupac Yupanqui. His father saved the life of a Spaniard named Ayala at the battle of Huarina, and ever afterwards adopted that name after his own. His son, the author, did the same. The work opens with a letter from the father, Martin Huaman Mallqui de Ayala, to Philip II, recommending his son's book to the royal notice. The author himself, Huaman Poma de Ayala, was chief of Lucanas.

The work commences with a history of the creation, the deluge, down to St. Peter's presentation of the keys to the Pope, about fifty-six pages, with excellent pen-and-ink sketches to illustrate the events. Then follow notices of the earliest traditions about Peruvian history, and the arrival of St. Bartholomew. The portraits of the twelve Incas are each accompanied by a page of description. The great value of the portraits consists in the excellent drawings of dresses and weapons. Portraits of the Ccoyas or Queens follow, and then those of fifteen famous captains. About sixty pages are devoted to the ordinances and laws, with a picture of the Inca surrounded by his councillors. Each month of the calendar is given, illustrated by pictures in which the exact shapes of agricultural implements are shown, among other things. Then come details of the *Huacas* or idols, divination, fasts, interments, and very graphic representations of the punishments for various offences. There is a chapter on the Virgins of the Sun with an illustration, and several Quichua harvest, hunting, dancing, and love songs. Huaman Poma next describes the palaces, and gives an account of the occupations of the people at various ages.

Then comes the conquest. The author gives pictures of Atahualpa, of Pizarro and Almagro, and of his own relations being roasted alive by Pizarro. There are a series of portraits of the eight first Viceroys, and of the later native chiefs in Spanish dress. Next a long series of pictures of cities in Peru, nearly all imaginary, and lists of post-houses, or *tambos*, on the various roads. But by far the most remarkable feature of this chronicle is an open and fearless attack on the cruel tyranny of the Spanish rule. The combined writer and artist spares neither priest nor corregidor. We see people being flogged, beaten with clubs, and hung up by the heels. There is a woman stripped naked and flogged because her tribute was two eggs short, shameful treatment of girls is depicted, inhuman flogging of children, forced marriages, and priests gambling with corregidors.

The author travelled all over Peru in some capacity, interceding for, and trying to protect, the unfortunate people. He was writing during thirty years, from 1583 to 1613. He concludes with an anticipation of the treatment of his book by the Christians of the world. 'Some,' he thinks, 'will weep, others will laugh, others will curse, others will commend him to God, others from rage will want to destroy the book. A few will want to have it in their hands.'

It is addressed to King Philip II, and the author had the temerity to take it down to Lima for transmission to Spain. He hoped to be appointed Protector of the Indians. We do not know what became of him. How the book, with all those damning illustrations, escaped destruction, and how it was ever allowed to be sent home, is a mystery! One would give much to know the fate of the author, so full of compassion for his ill-fated countrymen, diligent as a collector of information of all kinds, proud of his ancestry, a gifted artist, full of sympathy, fearless in the exposure of injustice and cruelty. Huaman Poma was a hero of whom any country might be proud. A vein of humour runs through his sketches. Their escape from destruction is little short of miraculous. At length this most important work is in good and sympathetic hands, and will be given to the world. It is, without exception, the most remarkable as well as the most interesting production of native genius that has come down to our time.

We have seen that the story of the Incas has been told by priests, soldiers, lawyers, by mestizos and by pure-blooded Indians. Seeing the same acts and events from different points of view, hearing them from various people, biased by prejudices which tend to obscure the truth, some desirous of securing accuracy, others thinking more of proving their case, some transparently honest, others less so in varied degrees,—it is evident that discrimination is called for after careful study. The following essays are the results of such study by one who has devoted many years of research to a most interesting and fascinating story.

CHAPTER II. THE MEGALITHIC AGE

THERE is a mystery still unsolved, on the plateau of Lake Titicaca, which, if stones could speak, would reveal a story of the deepest interest. Much of the difficulty in the solution of this mystery is caused by the nature of the region, in the present day, where the enigma still defies explanation. We must, therefore, first acquire some knowledge of the face of the country before we have the question, as it now stands, placed before us.

The great Cordilleras of the Andes, in latitude 14 28′ S., unite at the knot of Vilcañota, and then separate, forming the eastern Andes on one side, containing Illimani and Illampu (except Aconcagua and Huascaran, the loftiest measured peaks of the new world), and the maritime cordillera on the other. Between them there is an extensive and very lofty plateau, 13,000 to 14,000 feet above the sea, with the lake called Titicaca, or Inticaca, in its centre. Titicaca is the largest lake in South America. It was formerly much larger. The surface of the lake is 12,508 feet above the sea, that of the plateau being, on an average, several hundred feet higher..

The surrounding mountains form a region of frost and snow. The hardy llamas and alpacas live and breed amidst the tufts of coarse grass called *ychu*, and the graceful vicuñas can endure the rigorous climate at still higher elevations. Besides the grass, there is a lowly shrub called *tola*, which can be used as firewood. *Quinua*, belonging to the spinach family, can alone be raised at the higher elevations, yielding a small grain which, by itself, is insufficient to maintain human life.

The plateau itself, called the Collao, is by no means level. It is intersected by ranges of hills of no great height, and in the northern part the lofty rock of Pucara is a marked feature. Very hardy trees of three kinds, though stunted, are a relief to the landscape, and in some sheltered ravines they even form picturesque groves overshadowed by rocky heights. The tree at the highest elevations is called *queñua*; the two others, with gnarled rough trunks and branches, called *ccolli* and *quisuar* (*Oliva sylvestre* by the Spaniards, from a fancied resemblance of the leaves), are the only trees of the Titicaca plateau. Crops of potatoes are raised, forming the staple food, with the *oca* and some other edible roots. But cereals will not ripen, and the green barley is only used for fodder. The *yutu*, a kind of partridge, and a large rodent called *viscacha*, abound in the mountains, while the lake yields fish of various kinds, and is frequented by waterfowl.

Such a region is only capable of sustaining a scanty population of hardy mountaineers and labourers. The mystery consists in the existence of ruins of a great city on the southern side of the lake, the builders being entirely unknown.

The city covered a large area, built by highly skilled masons, and with the use of enormous stones. One stone is 36 feet long by 7, weighing 170 tons, another 26 feet by 16 by 6. Apart from the monoliths of ancient Egypt, there is nothing to equal this in any other part of the world. The movement and the placing of such monoliths point to a dense population, to an organised government, and consequently to a large area under cultivation, with arrangements for the conveyance of supplies from various directions. There must have been an organisation combining skill and intelligence with power and administrative ability.

The point next in interest to the enormous size of the stones is the excellence of the workmanship. The lines are accurately straight, the angles correctly drawn, the surfaces level. The upright monoliths have mortices and projecting ledges to retain the horizontal slabs in their places, which completed the walls. The carvings are complicated, and at the same time well arranged, and the ornamentation is accurately designed and executed. Not less striking are the statues with heads adorned with curiously shaped head-dresses. Flights of stone steps have recently been discovered, for the ancient city, now several miles from the lake, was once upon its borders. Remarkable skill on the part of the masons is shown by every fragment now lying about. Such are the angle-joints of a stone conduit; a window-frame of careful workmanship with nine apertures, all in one piece; and numerous niches and mouldings. There is ample proof of the very advanced stage reached by the builders in architectural art.

There are some particulars respecting the ruins in Oliva's history of Jesuits in Peru, obtained from an Indian named Catari, a *Quipucamayoc*, or reader of the *quipus*, who was living at Cochapampa in the end of the sixteenth century. It appears that Bartolomé Cervantes, a canon of Chuquisaca, gave to Oliva a manuscript dictated by Catari. The remarkable statement is here made that no judgment can be formed of the size of the ruined city, because nearly all was built underground. Professor Nestler of Prague has proceeded to Tiahuanacu with the object of making researches by the light of the account of Catari.

The famous monolithic doorway at Tiahuanacu has been fractured, probably by an earthquake. The lower part has not yet been excavated, so that it is not known whether the two sides are connected below or separate. The elaborate carving on the upper part may possibly hold the mystery. In the centre there is a square of seventeen-and-a-half inches, on which the principal figure is carved. The space is nearly square, surrounded by a border with billet ornaments. There are two round indentations for eyes, a nose, mouth, and three small holes on each cheek. The billet ornaments occur again on the sceptres and on the belt. Ornaments issue from the border round the head, consisting of twenty-two ribands ending in heads or circles. In the centre, at the top, there is a human head, on either side two ribands adorned with billets and ending in circles. At the angles there are longer ribands ending with the heads of beasts. These seven bands, including the human head, form the upper part of the rays round the greater head. On the sides there is a riband ending in a beast's head, and two rays ending in circles on either side of it, making a total of ten bands or rays on the sides of the head. Under the head the central band ends with a larger circle, having two smaller ones on either side of it. This makes a total of twenty-two ribands surrounding the head. It is not improbable that they may be intended to represent rays, like those of the sun, but their differences and arrangement also point to some symbolical meaning.

This central figure further has a riband passing round the neck and down to the belt, on either side of the breast. The parts on the breast have three divisions similarly marked on either side. On the upper one there are four small circles, on the next a small circle and two figures like a V, and on the lower division there is a diamond-shaped figure with another within it. I am inclined to think that these curious carvings are intended to represent emblems of months or seasons. In the centre of the breast, between the bands, there is a conventional ornament of two bands ending in heads of birds, and over them another symbol of a month or season. The belt round the figure consists of a band with three billets, terminating at each end with a beast's head.

The arms issue from the sides in a curve, with human heads hanging from the elbows. The hands, showing three fingers and a thumb, grasp sceptres. Below the hands the two sceptres are exactly the same, consisting of three joints, each with a billet, and ending in a bird's head. Above the hands the sceptres differ. The one on the right consists of five joints with billets and the appearance of a small bird. The one on the left is divided into two, ending with heads of birds.

Below the belt there is a band, whence hangs a fringe of six human heads. The central figure terminates at the knees, just above an elaborately carved ornament which is supposed to have represented a throne. It consists of bands ending in twelve birds' heads, and at the sides the composition terminates in a large beast's head, with a peculiar ornament in front of the mouth. There are three squares, the two outer ones having inner squares, and issuing from them another square, with short bands, ending in a circle and inner circle, on either side.

On either side of the central figure there are forty-eight figures kneeling to it, sixteen with the heads of birds and thirty-two with human heads. All are winged, all are crowned, and all hold sceptres. The bird-headed worshippers have sceptres like the one in the central figure's left hand, while the sceptres of the human-headed worshippers are the same as those in the central figure's right hand. The bird-headed figures have ornamental bands with terminals of fish heads, and the human-headed figures throughout have bands ending in birds' heads.

It is difficult to avoid the conclusion that the central figure is intended to represent the deity having jurisdiction over all human beings on the one hand, and over the animal creation on the other.

Below the rows of worshippers there is a beautifully carved border consisting of double lines ending with birds' heads, surrounding human heads with borders of joints and billets, surmounted in one by five bands ending in circles, in another by four fish heads, in another by an armed human figure.

There is no sign of sculpture nor of any knowledge of proportion in designing a human figure; but at the same time there are indications of very remarkable skill and taste in the masonic art. The ornamentation is accurately designed and executed, and the style of art is well adapted for symbolical representation. The tendency is to straight lines and rectangles, not to curves.

This, then, is the mystery. A vast city containing palace, temple, judgment-hall, or whatever fancy may reconstruct among the ruins, with statues, elaborately carved stones, and many triumphs of the masonic art, was built in a region where corn will not ripen, and which could not possibly support a dense population. It is quite certain that, in the time of the Incas, the people were absolutely ignorant of the origin and history of these edifices. They were to them, as they are to us, mysterious ruins. The statues gave rise to a myth referring to a former creation by the deity, rising from the lake, of men and women who, for disobedience, were turned into stone. This was to account for the statues. The name of Tiahuanacu is modern. It is said that an Inca happened to receive a message when visiting the ruins, and he compared the rapidity of the runner to that of the swiftest animal known to him: 'Tia, huanacu,' he said ('Be seated, huanacu'), and the place has since had that name. When the Spaniards arrived the ruins were very much in the same state as they are now. The Jesuit Acosta, who took measurements of the stones, speaks of them as ruins of very ancient buildings. Cieza de Leon mentions two gigantic statues which were much weathered and showed marks of great antiquity. An old schoolfellow of Garcilasso, in writing to him, described the ruins as very ancient.

The builders may best be described as a megalithic people in a megalithic age, an age when cyclopean stones were transported, and cyclopean edifices raised.

The great antiquity is shown by the masonry and symbolical carving, but this is not the only proof that Andean civilisation dates back into a far distant past. The advances made by the Andean people in agriculture and in the domestication of animals must have been proceeding from a very remote period. Maize had been brought to a high state of cultivation, and this must have been the result of careful and systematic labour during many centuries. The cultivation must have been commenced at so remote a time that it is not even certainly known from what wild plant the original maize was derived. The wild potato, however, is known. It is a small tuber, about the size of a filbert, which has scarcely increased in size after a century of careful cultivation. Yet the Andean people, after many centuries of such cultivation, produced excellent potatoes of several kinds, for each of which they had a name. The same may be said of the *oca* and *quinua* crops. The agricultural achievements of Andean man are evidence of the vast antiquity of his race in the same region. The domestication of the llama and alpaca furnish additional evidence of this antiquity. There is no wild llama. The huanacu and vicuña are different animals. It must have been centuries before the llama was completely domesticated, carrying burdens, yielding its wool for clothing and its flesh for food. Individuals are of various colours, as is usual with domesticated animals, while the wild huanacus have fleeces of the same colour. The domestication of the alpaca must have taken an equally long period, and called for even greater skill and care. There is no wild alpaca, and the tame animal is dependent on man for the performance of most of its functions. It must have taken ages to bring the silken fleeces to such perfection.

There is thus good reason for assigning very great antiquity to the civilisation of the megalithic people. Another deduction from the premises is that there must have been a dense population for working quarries, moving the cyclopean monoliths from a distance and placing them, as well as for cultivation and the provision of supplies for the workers. This suggests extensive dominions, and some movement of the people.

We only have tradition to indicate the direction whence the megalithic people came. I am quite in agreement with Dr. Brinton that 'the culture of the Andean race is an indigenous growth, wholly self-developed, and owing none of its germs to any other races.' Mr. Squier came to the same conclusion as regards Peru, and Mr. Maudslay as regards the Mayas of Central America. There were doubtless movements among the Andean tribes, gradual progress extending over vast periods of time, and an influx from some direction to form the megalithic empire. But from what direction? Tradition points to the south, to Charcas and Tucuman, and to countries beyond the southern tropic, as the sources of its population. It is interesting to find Garcilasso de la Vega, in one of his letters, describing himself as an 'Antarctic Indian.' Cieza de Leon, the earliest author to collect native traditions, tells us that the people came from the south. Betanzos also makes the civilisers advance from the south. Salcamayhua says that all the nations of Peru came from the south, and settled in the various regions as they advanced. Molina has the same tradition. Montesinos mentions a great invasion from the south in the very earliest times, later the records tell of the arrival of an army from Tucuman, and he tells of a third great invasion from the south when his 62nd King was reigning. On this point there is practical unanimity. The great population, of the existence of which the Tiahuanacu ruins bear silent testimony, represents a series of movements from the south.

The Tiahuanacu ruins also point to extensive dominion, and to ascertain its extent and locality we must seek for similar cyclopean work, and for similar masonic skill in carving, in other parts of Peru.

In Cuzco there is a cyclopean building in the *Calle del Triunfo*, with a huge monolith known as the 'stone of twelve corners.' Some portions of the ancient remains at Ollantay-tampu are megalithic work, as well as the '*Inca-misana*' and '*Ñusta-tiana*,' hewn out of the solid rock. But the grandest and most imposing work of the megalithic builders was the fortress at Cuzco. The Sacsahuaman hill, on which the fortress stood overlooking the city, was practically inaccessible on two sides, and easily defensible on another. But the eastern face was exposed to easy approach, and here the great cyclopean work was constructed. It consists of three parallel walls, 330 yards in length each, with 21 advancing and retiring angles, so that at every point an attack could be enfiladed by defenders. The outer wall, at its salient angles, has stones of the following dimensions: 14 ft. high by 12; another, 10 ft. by 6. There must have been some good cause for the erection of this marvellous defensive work of which we know nothing. Its origin is as unknown as that of the Tiahuanacu ruins. The Incas knew nothing. Garcilasso refers to towers, walls, and gates built by the Incas, and even gives the names of the architects; but these were later defences built within the great cyclopean fortress. The outer lines must be attributed to the megalithic age. There is nothing of the kind which can be compared to them in any other part of the world. At Chavin, in the valley of the Marañon, there is cyclopean work, and also in Chachapoyas.

In seeking for indications of the megalithic age to be found in the elaborate carving of stones, we at once turn to the great monoliths at Concacha, near Abancay, and to the stone of Chavin. At Concacha the huge sacrificial stone is of limestone, about 20 ft. long by 14 by 12. It is carved in channels for leading away liquids, and in other forms. It points to the megalithic age, as does the circular stone with much fine workmanship in *alto relievo*, the great seats cut out of monoliths, and the flight of stone steps to form an artificial cascade. On the Chavin stone we again have the Deity holding two sceptres, as at Tiahuanacu.

This stone was found in about 1840, in the parish of Chavin de Huantar, in the province of Huari, and within the valley of the Marañon. Here there is a curious Inca ruin, known as the Pucara de Chavin. The stone had fallen from the ruins above, but it does not follow that it was the same age as the ruins. It was probably once part of a much more ancient edifice, afterwards used to adorn the more recent Inca fortress. In 1874 the stone was taken to Lima by order of the government, where it now may be seen.

The Chavin stone is of diorite, 25 ft. long by 2 ft. 4 in. The carving is very elaborate, and covers the whole length and breadth of the stone. The principal figure occupies the lower half of the stone. The ornamentation is richer and more confused than that on the Tiahuanacu monolith. The head is still square, the chief difference being in the large mouth with teeth and tusks. The rays are not all round the head, but only on the sides, three in number. They are more curved, and end in heads resembling those of serpents. This was the conventional ornament of the later megalithic school of art. At Tiahuanacu the heads are clearly those of beasts, birds, and fish. On the Chavin stone they are all the same, like heads of snakes. But I incline to believe that the latter are merely conventional heads to finish off the bands or rays. Two also come out of each of the knees of the figure.

As in the Tiahuanacu figure there are two arms, with hands grasping sceptres. But on the Chavin stone the sceptres, though much thicker and more elaborately carved, have lost their symbolic meaning. Each has two long bands terminating in heads.

Above the central figure of the Chavin stone there is a richly ornamented composition. Along the centre there are rows of teeth with tusks and three heads on either side, then curves, tusks alternating with bands ending in volutes. At the sides there are 34 long bands, 17 on each side, ending alternately with volutes and heads. At the very top two bands are twisted round each other, terminating with heads. The whole composition, above the central figure, seems to represent an immense and richly ornamented head-dress.

The same general idea appears to prevail in both the central figures at Tiahuanacu and on the Chavin stone. They represent the genius of the same people, and the same civilisation, though at different periods, the Chavin stone being the latest. In both the pervading idea is of a figure of the Deity grasping a sceptre in each hand. The bands or rays terminating with heads or with circles and volutes are the same in both. At Tiahuanacu all the parts of the carving appear to have a symbolical meaning. The artist avoided all curves, preferring straight lines and correctly drawn rectangles. Everything seems to have an intention or a meaning. In the Chavin stone the conception is more confused, and there is much that is more ornate, but apparently conventional and unmeaning.

The two compositions, it may be concluded, are the work of the same people, with the same cult, the same art, and the same traditions, but with an interval of perhaps a century or two between them. There must once have been other stones of the same character. One was probably at Cacha, another at Cuzco, belonging to the same megalithic age. If they had not been destroyed, we could trace the transition from the earlier and simpler style, full of meaning, at Tiahuanacu, to the more elaborate and corrupt work on the Chavin stone.

Guided by the existence of megalithic ruins and by the carved stones, we are led to the tentative conclusion that the ancient empire extended its sway over the Andean regions from an unknown distance south of Tucuman to Chachapoyas, with Tiahuanacu (for want of the real name) as its centre of rule and of thought. We may also entertain two provisional conclusions, one of them touching the great antiquity of the megalithic civilisation, and the other with reference to the area over which it prevailed.

But we must return to the most difficult part of the problem, namely, the climatic conditions. How could such a region as is described at the beginning of this essay, where corn cannot ripen, sustain the population of a great city over 12,000 ft. above the level of the sea? Could the elevation have been less? Is such an idea beyond the bounds of possibility? The height is now 12,500 ft. above the sea level, in latitude 16 22′ S.

The recent studies of southern geology and botany lead to the belief in a connection between South America and the Antarctic continental lands. But at a remote geological period there was no South America, only three land masses, separated by great sea inlets, a Guiana, a Brazil, and a La Plata island. There were no Andes. Then came the time when the mountains began to be upheaved. The process appears to have been very slow, gradual, and long continued. The Andes did not exist at all in the Jurassic, or even in the cretaceous period. Comparatively speaking, the Andes are very modern. The bones of a mastodon have been discovered at Ulloma, in Bolivia, which is now 13,000 ft. above the sea. But such an animal could not have existed at such an elevation. Then, again, in the deserts of Tarapaca, embedded in the sides of ravines, there are numerous skeletons of gigantic ant-eaters, animals whose habitat is in a dense forest. When they lived, the deserts in which their bones are found must have been covered with trees. It is the height of the Andes, wringing all moisture out of the trade wind, which makes Tarapaca a desert. When the Andes were lower, the trade wind could carry its moisture over them to the strip of coast land which is now an arid desert, producing arboreal vegetation and the means of supporting gigantic ant-eaters. When mastodons lived at Ulloma, and ant-eaters in Tarapaca, the Andes, slowly rising, were some two or three thousands of feet lower than they are now. Maize would then ripen in the basin .of Lake Titicaca, and the site of the ruins of Tiahuanacu could support the necessary population. If the megalithic builders were living under these conditions, the problem is solved. If this is geologically impossible, the mystery remains unexplained.

We have indications of the megalithic civilisation, of the direction whence it came, of its great antiquity, of the extent of the ancient empire, deduced from the ruins and carved stones, and of the religious feeling, shown by a central figure worshipped by men and the brute creation. We know nothing more about the mysterious megalithic people, unless any light can be thrown on them by a consideration of the long list of kings, which will form the subject of the next chapter.

CHAPTER III. THE LIST OF KINGS

A LONG list of a hundred kings of Peru, including the Incas, was given in the writings of Fernando Montesinos, who was in Peru from 1629 to 1642. The writer was credulous and uncritical, and his information was collected a century after the conquest, when all the instructed Indians who could remember the days of the Incas had passed away. Little credence has, therefore, been given to the list hitherto. But Dr. Gonzalez de la Rosa has recently adduced good reasons for the belief that Montesinos merely copied the list of kings, which was well known long before his time. It was compiled, almost certainly, by Blas Valera, when learned men of the time of the Incas were still living, Valera himself being the son of an Indian mother, and the language of the Incas being his mother tongue. The list, therefore, comes to us on the highest authority, as a genuine tradition of the learned men of Inca times. It is thus placed in quite a different position, and calls for serious consideration.

The list of kings, assuming Blas Valera to have been the compiler, was derived from the ancient *quipu* records, expounded by learned men of the time of the Incas, called AMAUTAS and QUIPUCAMAYOCS, who had charge of these records previous to the Spanish conquest. It is conceivable that such records may have been preserved. The ancient Peruvians, like other races in the same stage of civilisation, were genealogists, and had an unusual number of words to distinguish relationships. The chronology of the list, as shown by the length of reigns, is not exaggerated. It gives an average of twenty-five to twenty-seven years for each reign. It is true that, if the whole represents a succession of fathers and sons, it would take us back to 950 B.C. But a large allowance may be made for successions of brothers or cousins, and for repetitions, which would bring the initial date down to about 200 B.C.

The list commences with the names of the Deity, ILLA TICI UIRACOCHA. We are told that the first word, ILLA, means 'Light.' TICI means 'foundation or beginning of things.' The word UIRA is said to be a corruption of PIRUA, meaning the 'depository or store-house of creation.' But here there is some confusion. For the name of the first recorded king is given as PIRUA PACCARI MANCO; and the Deity is said to be his God—the God of Pirua. In modern Quichua *Pirua* means a granary or store-house. UIRA is the store-house or depository of all things—of creation. The ordinary meaning of COCHA is a lake, but here it is said to signify an abyss—profundity. The whole meaning of the words would be 'The splendour, the foundation, the creator, the infinite God.' The word YACHACHIC was occasionally added—'the Teacher.'

It may well be that the Tiahuanacu carving was an effort to give expression to this idea of the Deity. The names show the sublimity of thought attained by the ancient Peruvians in their conception of a Supreme Being—the infinite cause, the fundamental principle, the light of the world, the great teacher.

The first recorded king, whose Deity is thus described, was Pirua Paccari Manco. His dynasty, which may be called the Pirua dynasty, would include the first eighteen kings in the list, who may possibly be megalithic sovereigns. It may be that some glimmer of light may be afforded by their names. They yield twenty-one words, of which sixteen have meanings in modern Quichua. Three of these are titles which occur frequently. These are CCAPAC, occurring eleven times; YUPANQUI, four times; and PACHACUTI twice in the Pirua dynasty. CCAPAC means 'rich,' but applied to a sovereign it conveys the idea of being 'rich in all virtues.' The word YUPANQUI is an equivalent; literally, 'you may count,' but here it is 'you may count for being possessed of all virtues.' The word PACHACUTI is composed of the two words PACHA, 'time,' or the 'world,' and CUTINI, 'I turn, change back, or reform.' It was applied to sovereigns in whose reigns there was a change in the calendar, or great reforms, or some important event.

These three words were titles, the others are the actual names of sovereigns. Those which belong to the Quichua language have such meanings as princely, august, strong, the scatterer, sun, dawn, crystal, music, a landmark, a brick, a serpent, and a leveller of ground (*cozque*), whence the name Cuzco. There is also one name after a locality—Huascar—which also means a cable.

Finally, there are three names which have no meaning in Quichua (with the exception of *Pirua*, a granary), and may be archaic, possibly megalithic. These are AYAR, MANCO, PAULLU. Paullu may possibly be a name taken from a locality.

It has been suggested by Don Vicente Lopez that the Pirua dynasty ended with the eighteenth king, and that a new AMAUTA dynasty commenced with the nineteenth. His only reason for this idea is that the successor of the eighteenth king is only called his heir, and not, as heretofore, his son and heir. This is a mistake, for five other Piruan kings are not said to be sons of their predecessors. The theory is, however, convenient, and there is perhaps a better reason for its adoption. After the eighteenth king the title AMAUTA first appears, and is given to thirteen out of the forty-six succeeding kings who are supposed to form the Amauta dynasty. The name was given to learned men, keepers of the records and revisers of the calendar. The Magian dynasty in Persia, when the same class seized the government, was much more short-lived. The words ATAUCHI and AUQUI first appear as titles in the Amauta dynasty, the one meaning a married prince, and the other also a prince in Quichua, but a father in the southern dialect. There are also the names RAYMI and HUQUIZ, which have no meaning in Quichua. It is said that the king with the former name gave it to the festivals he instituted, while King HUQUIZ gave his name to the intercalary days. The name HUANACAURI occurs twice, and CAURI alone, once. This word is of peculiar interest because it was given to one of the most sacred idols of the Incas, near Cuzco. It has no meaning, though it has a Quichua appearance. *Huan* means 'with'; *Huanac*, 'a warning.' *Caura* is a laden llama in the southern dialect. But it is useless to speculate. Two kings took the sacred name of the Deity. One was called UILCAÑOTA, after the place where he won a victory over invaders. The other personal names which are not in the Pirua list all have meanings in Quichua, except two or three which are corrupt. Their meanings are light, fire, gold, sacred, a chief, a boy, a beam, a head-dress, left-handed, blood, tobacco, a falcon, a dove, and a foot. There is a name, MARASCO, which is suggestive, for MARAS was the name of one of the tribes mentioned as following the children of the sun in the Paccari-tampu myth, which will be the subject of the next essay.

The end of the early civilisation is stated to have been caused by a great invasion from the south, when the reigning king was defeated and killed in a battle near Pucara, in the Collao. The whole country broke up into a number of petty tribes, and barbarism returned, with a vicious state of society and intestine feuds. This story may well represent an historical fact. A remnant of the AMAUTAS, with their followers, took refuge in a district called TAMPU-TOCCO, near the great river Apurimac. Here the tradition of the Deity was preserved, and some remnants of the old civilisation. Elsewhere the religion became degraded each chief adopting some natural object as his ancestor, and worshipping it instead of the old Deity. The more civilised kings of Tampu-tocco declared themselves to be children of the sun.

There are twenty-seven kings of Tampu-tocco in the list, who may cover a period of 650 years. Few new names appear. The most important is ROCCA, which seems to be archaic, having no meaning in Quichua. Another is RANTI ALLI (corruptly ARANTIAL). RANTI means a deputy, and ALLI, good. Other names which have not occurred before are HUAYNA, a youth; ATAU, fortune of war; Tocco, a window; HUARI, and HUISPA, corrupt; and CUIS. CUY means a guinea-pig. The last Tampu-tocco king was INTI MAYTA CCAPAC, the eighth PACHACUTI. The word MAYTA occurs first in his name, and a meaning has been given to it. MAY is where, TA, through. Perhaps a question 'Whither go I?'—recalling the last verses of the Emperor Hadrian.

After this examination of the list of kings, the question arises whether it throws any light on the problem of the megalithic age and the Tiahuanacu ruins. I am disposed to think that we may obtain a glimmering of light from it. The record of the names and attributes of the ancient Deity is important. The destruction of the old civilisation, in a great battle, and the subsequent disruption, with the preservation of some remnant of civilisation and religion at Tampu-tocco, the place of refuge, explains what follows. The superiority and predominance of the so-called children of the sun is thus explained. It may be that the PIRUA and AMAUTA dynasties may possibly represent the sovereigns of the megalithic empire. Its decline and fall was followed by centuries of barbarism, so that the people had almost forgotten its existence, while the tribes of the Collao were probably of another race, descendants of invaders. As the Bible and the literature and art of Greece and Rome were preserved through centuries of barbarism by the monasteries, so the religion and civilisation of the megalithic empire were preserved through centuries of barbarism by the Amautas of Tamputocco. In one case the dark period was succeeded by the age of the Renaissance, in the other by the enlightened rule of the Incas.

CHAPTER IV. THE PACCARI-TAMPU MYTH

THERE is a myth which was told to all the Spanish authors by their native informants, and is retailed by them with some variations, the most authentic version being that officially received from the Incas by Sarmiento. While the Titicaca myth was obviously invented to account for the ancient ruins and statues, and has no historical value, the Paccari-tampu myth is as certainly the outcome of a real tradition, and is the fabulous version of a distant historical event.

We are taken to the country of refuge at TAMPU-TOCCO, where one side is protected from invasion by the deep gorge of the Apurimac. The fugitives of long ages back had multiplied. The descendants were more civilised, therefore more powerful than their neighbours, and the time had come for the acquisition of better and more extensive territory. The idea of windows in the following myth was perhaps suggested by the word TOCCO, the meaning of which is a window in Quichua. The district is called PACCARI-TAMPU, or the 'Tavern of the Dawn,' in the legend, and TAMPU-TOCCO is the hill with the three openings or windows, called MARAS, SUTIC, and CCAPAC.

The legend relates how, out of the MARAS window came a tribe with the same name, from the SUTIC window came a tribe named TAMPU. Out of the central CCAPAC window came four august personages, all bearing the title of AYAR, a designation of several of the ancient kings. There were MANCO, the princely; Ayar AUCA, the fighting or joyful Ayar; CACHI, the salt Ayar; and UCHU, the pepper Ayar. With them were their four wives, OCCLO, the august princess; HUACO, the warlike princess; IPACURA, the elder aunt; and RAUA.

The four children of the sun, with their four wives, consulted together and came to a momentous decision: 'We are born strong and wise, and with the people who will follow us we are powerful. We will go forth to seek more fertile lands, and when we find them we will subdue the people, making war upon all who do not receive us as their Lords.'

There was a considerable force at their command besides the two tribes who are said to have issued from the windows on the hill of TAMPU-TOCCO, named MARAS and TAMPU. Eight other *ayllus* or lineages were mustered under the banner of the Ayars, whose names were preserved. The CHAVIN tribe served under the salt Ayar. With it were the ARAYRACA tribe, the CUYCUSA, the MASCA, the URU, and the SAÑOC. The TARPUNTAY was probably the priestly and sacrificial caste, while the HUACAY TAQUI *ayllu* was also a religious body conducting ceremonials and musical festivals. The gathering of these ten tribes together seems to have been a veritable exodus under the leadership of the Ayars. For they not only took with them their arms, but also their movable property, wives and children.

Their way was north-east for not more than twenty-five miles, for no doubt Cuzco was their goal from the beginning, well known to them as a desirable central position where megalithic buildings gave evidence of former occupation by the ancient civilisers. Starting from their homes at TAMPU-TOCCO their movements were slow and deliberate, even stopping to sow and reap. The Ayar Manco was the leader. He took with him a golden staff. When the soil was so fertile that its whole length sank into the rich mould, there was to be the final resting-place. He also had with him a bird like a falcon, carried in a hamper, which all the people looked upon as sacred. It does not appear whether it was alive or artificial, but it was the Ayar's familiar spirit called HUAUQUI, or brother.

Their first march took this army of empire builders to a place called Huanacancha, where there was a long halt, and the next sojourn was at Tampuquiru and Pallata, contiguous villages. Here they remained for several years sowing and reaping crops. But they were not satisfied with it, and moved on to another valley, called HAIS QUISRU.

The story proceeds to relate the way in which Manco got rid of his three brothers, so as to rule alone. The salt Ayar is described as so cruel and oppressive that the brothers feared that their followers would desert and leave them alone. He was so dexterous with the sling, and so strong that with each shot he pulled down a mountain and filled up a ravine. The existing ravines on the line of march were made by the salt Ayar in hurling rocks. The Inca Garcilasso tells us that the meaning of salt (CACHI), as applied to this Ayar, signifies instruction in rational life. His teaching must have been rather vigorous. We are told that his brothers feared him, and conspired to take his life.

They made a plot alike cunning and cruel. They called the salt Ayar to them and told him that some precious insignia had been forgotten, and left in the cave whence they came, called CCAPAC-TOCCO. These were the golden vases called TUPAC CUSI, and the NAPA, a sacred figure of a llama. They said that it would be for the good of all if he would go back and fetch them. At first he refused, but the strong-minded MAMA HUACO rebuked him with stinging words: 'How is it that there should be such cowardice in so strong a youth as you are?' she exclaimed. 'Get ready for the journey, and do not fail to return to Tampu-tocco, and do as you are desired.' He was shamed by these words, and set out with a companion named Tampu-chacay, who was an accomplice of the fratricides. When they arrived the salt Ayar entered the cave to fetch the treasures, which were not really there. His treacherous companion, with great celerity, rolled a rock against the opening and sat upon it, so that the salt Ayar might remain inside and die there. The outraged prince exerted all his mighty strength to move the rock. His cries made the mountains tremble. But all was of no avail. With his last breath he denounced the traitor, declaring that he should be turned into a stone and never return to report the success of his crime. To this day the traitor stone may be seen by the side of the Ccapac-tocco. The salt Ayar was thus disposed of. Next came the turn of the pepper Ayar.

The army of the Ayars continued their very deliberate advance, and came to a place called Quirirmanta, only a few miles from the valley of Cuzco. Here there was a hill which, according to Sarmiento, was afterwards called HUANACAURI. According to the legend, the brothers saw a sacred HUACA or idol on the hill, and proposed to take it away with them. The pepper Ayar was induced to approach it, and when he came in contact with the idol he was himself converted into stone. He just had time to say: 'Go, happy brothers. When you celebrate the *Huarachicu*, I shall be adored as the father of the young knights, for I must remain here for ever.' Garcilasso explains that the name of pepper (UCHU) was applied to this Ayar as symbolically meaning the delight experienced from leading a rational life. HUANACAURI or HUAYNA-CAPTIY became one of the most sacred HUACAS of the Peruvians. The word seems to have reference to the great festival when the youths received a sort of knighthood, the ceremony being performed near the *Huaca*. HUAYNA means a youth. *Cauri* is corrupt and has no meaning, but *Captiy* is the present subjunctive of the auxiliary verb. Here the unfortunate pepper Ayar was kept in memory, and received adoration at the great annual festival of arming the youths, for many generations.

Ayar Manco had now disposed of two of his brothers. The turn of the joyful or fighting Ayar was to come next. Meanwhile the march continued *festina lente*; and two years were passed in sowing and reaping at a place called Matahua, just within the Cuzco valley. Then it is related that Ayar Manco hurled his golden staff as far as Huanaypata, where it sank into the earth. By this they knew that the land was fertile and suited for settlement. But first the joyful Ayar must be disposed of. A pile of stones was in sight, where the temple of the sun afterwards stood. Manco told his last remaining brother, who was winged, that he must fly thither and take possession of the territory. The joyful Ayar did so, and when he sat on the mount, lo and behold! he was turned into a stone. This cairn or mound was called Cuzco, whence the name of the future city. The word means literally a clod of earth, or hard, unirrigated land. *Cuzquini* is to level or break clods of earth.

Whether the three Ayars were disposed of in this miraculous way, or whether their lives were taken without a disturbance of the laws of nature, Manco now had no rival. He occupied a strong position with his army, near the joyous Ayar's fatal Cuzco, and forcibly subdued the Alcavisas and other former settlers in the valley.

This Paccari-tampu myth is, I believe, founded on an important historical event. It records the march of those descendants of the ancient civilisers who took refuge at Tampu-tocco. They were empire builders marching to Cuzco, with their religious beliefs and ceremonies, their insignia of royalty, their traditions of laws and customs, and their household gods.

The fertile vale of Cuzco, several miles in length, and surrounded by mountains, is in latitude 13 30′ S. and 11,380 ft. above the level of the sea. Over its site rises the imposing hill of Sacsahuaman, with the ancient cyclopean fortress on the eastern side. This famous mount is separated from the hills on either side by deep ravines, down which two torrents flow, called the Huatanay and Tulumayu. Beaching the level ground which forms the site of Cuzco, they often overflowed their banks, causing swamps and injuring the land. Eventually they form a junction, and the united stream flows down the valley to join the Vilcamayu. It was at the junction of the torrents, about a mile from the foot of the Sacsahuaman, that Manco established his settlement. Here he erected the House of the Sun, called INTI-CACHA, but for a long time it was more a fortress than a temple. He and his successors subdued the former inhabitants of the valley, and the ten tribes from Tampu-tocco occupied their lands. These *ayllus*, or tribes, formed the fighting strength of the restored rule. Some of them, as the dominion extended, went further afield. The Maras tribe gave its name to the village of Maras, on the plateau overlooking the lovely vale of Vilcamayu. The Uru tribe was established at Urupampa, in the vale itself; and the Tampu tribe further down the same valley.

The date of the event recorded in the Paccaritampu myth may be placed at about four centuries before the Spanish conquest, in 1100 A.D. or thereabouts. Sarmiento places it at 565 A.D., by making each generation cover a century.

There is practical unanimity among all authorities with regard to the names of the four first successors of Manco. They were SINCHI ROCCA, LLOQUE YUPANQUI, MAYTA CCAPAC, and CCAPAC YUPANQUI. Most of these names are merely titles. The actual names are ROCCA, LLOQUE, and MAYTA. For the fourth only titles are given, and no personal name. The kings continued to live within the fortified INTI-CANCHA, dividing the land between the torrents into four quarters, to be occupied by their followers: namely QUINTI-CANCHA, or the angular place, where the torrents join; CHUMPI-CANCHA, or the place of stone heaps, perhaps buildings; SAYRI-CANCHA, or the place where the *Sayri* plant was cultivated; and YARAMPUY-CANCHA, another place for cultivation. These four kings undertook no great enterprise. Mayta Ccapac alone showed any energy, by finally subjugating the tribes in the Cuzco valley. The kings at the Inti-cancha were respected by the surrounding chiefs as children of the sun, and for their superior knowledge and civilisation. Envoys were sent to them, some with submission, and they wisely cemented alliances by marriages with daughters of their more powerful neighbours. The marriages with sisters was a much later custom of their prouder and more imperially minded successors.

Apparently these early successors of Manco, owing to a certain superiority, occupied a position of priority, scarcely of suzerainty, over a very loose confederacy of surrounding tribes speaking the same language. But this was not what was contemplated by the Ayar Manco, who had filled the minds of his tribes with ambitious ideas. There was a feeling of unrest and discontent, the very opportunity to be seized by a highly gifted adventurer, if time should produce one.

CHAPTER V. RISE OF THE INCAS

THERE was a feeling of unrest among the descendants of the conquering tribes led by the Ayars to Cuzco. Vice was unchecked, the leaders of the people remained inert in the Inti-cancha, and no progress was made. Yet the people themselves were still vigorous, only needing a resolute chief, with a genius for command, to guide and direct their destinies.

Among the discontented there was an ambitious lady, said to have been of the blood-royal, who, in consultation with her sister, one of the most noted sorceresses of that day, resolved to effect a revolution. Her name was SIUYACU, or the 'gradually increasing ring.' She was shrewd, cautious, and determined.

Her son Rocca was to be the instrument to effect the revolution she contemplated for the good of her people. He was a youth in his twentieth year, well formed, handsome, valiant, and with a mind filled with lofty ideals. Already he was the leader of the young men who were discontented, and among his intimates he was called INCA or Lord.

The lady SIUYACU thus opened the subject to her son. 'My son,' she began, ' you have a knowledge of the very happy estate enjoyed by our ancestors, when they occupied themselves in military exercises, and lived in conformity with the will of our great father the sun, and of the Supreme Creator ILLA TICI UIRA-COCHA. By this path the city flourished, there was a succession of many kings, the realm was extended, the course of events was prosperous, and we always triumphed over our enemies, of which things our *quipus* are full. All this is now changed. The country is in the miserable state in which you see it. But I have determined that you shall be king. I trust in the aid of the Supreme Creator, that he will favour my plans, and I trust that you, by your valour and wisdom, will be the Restorer of the city and the kingdom to its ancient prosperity.'

She ceased. Tears flowed from her eyes as she waited anxiously for her son's reply. There was a long pause. Rocca appeared to be deep in thought. After a time the valiant youth delivered his answer. 'Mother and Lady!' he said, 'what you have proposed must be for the common good of all the realm. As to what you have said of me, I dutifully accept your judgment. I declare to you that I am ready to give my life a thousand times that your noble aspirations may be fulfilled.'

His mother was satisfied, for she knew the resolution of her son if he once undertook an enterprise, that with him there would be no turning back, and she was impressed with his wisdom in accepting counsel, and with his capacity in the execution of a carefully prepared scheme. She embraced him, declaring that she hoped no less of his valour and high spirit. She impressed him with the absolute necessity of silence, and charged him to follow exactly the instructions he would receive from herself and his aunt, the sorceress.

The lady SIUYACU next gave an account to her sister of this interview with her son, dwelling on the attention he had given to her words, and on his willingness to enter into her plans. His attitude promised success, and the sisters determined to take action without delay. The sorceress employed certain artisans, who were sworn to secrecy, to beat out a great number of square pieces of fine gold, with small holes perforated at each corner. They then sewed them on to a long garment, reaching from the neck to the heels, with numerous brilliant precious stones between the golden plates. The whole shone like the rays of the sun. The sisters then made several trials with the youth, to decide upon the way in which he should appear. At last they took him to a cave called Chingana, in the side of the Sacsahuaman hill, which overlooks the city. They dressed him in the gold-embroidered robe, and told him, at the end of four days, to appear at noon, on the height that dominates the whole city, so that the people might see him, and then to return to his hiding-place, where sufficient food had been provided.

The two sisters then declared to the people that, while their son and nephew, INCA ROCCA, was sleeping in the house, the sun came down and carried him up to heaven enveloped in its rays, saying that he would soon return as king and favoured child of the great luminary. The solemn statement was confirmed by six members of the family who were witnesses. Partly on account of these assurances, partly because they had long looked upon Rocca as a child of destiny, most of the people believed the story. If there were any doubts they were soon dispelled.

Great numbers of people came from far and near to hear the news. On the fourth day sacrifices were offered to the sun from early morning, with earnest prayers that the youth might be restored.

Immense crowds were in the open space before the Inti-cancha. The hour of noon arrived. The busy hum of voices ceased. There was an awed silence, for there, on the summit of the Sacsahuaman hill, in the sight of all men, stood a golden figure glittering in the sun's rays. Then it suddenly disappeared, but thousands had seen it. The effect was indescribable. It must be Rocca, without doubt, and the sun had shown him, in answer to their prayers.

At nightfall the lady SIUYACU was at the Chingana, instructing her son to appear again, in the same way, at the end of two days, and then hide himself as before. During the interval the people were in suspense, and full of anxiety to see the end of such wonderful events. After two days the golden figure was again seen, for a few moments, on the summit of the Sacsahuaman hill. The feelings of the people were wrought up to the highest pitch of excitement. SIUYACU seized the fateful moment. She announced that the Supreme Creator, ILLA TICI, had told her to go to the cave Chingana, where she would find her son. He was to be taken to the temple, where the people would hear the divine message from his lips, and must obey him in all things as one inspired by the Deity. The people prepared themselves by dressing as for a festival, amidst the most enthusiastic rejoicings. Then nearly the whole population, led by the lady SIUYACU, rushed up the hill, along the walls of the megalithic fortress, to the Chingana cave. Under a carved stone they found young Rocca reclining, apparently asleep. He awoke, and, rising to his feet, he told the people, with an air of great authority, that they must repair to the temple, where, by command of his father the sun, he would give them the message he had received.

The return of the people was more solemn. There was an awed silence. Rocca was seated on a golden throne within the temple. The vast crowd was eager to hear the message. A profound silence prevailed throughout the vast concourse of listeners as he rose to speak. These are said to have been his words: 'No one can doubt, my friends, the special love which my father the sun feels for us. When he weakened the power of this realm so that it fell to pieces, he took care to provide a remedy. It was vice and sloth which consumed its grandeur, and reduced it almost to a vanishing point. Our policy was turned into a system of each man being his own master, leaving us to be satisfied with the thought that once we had a government. The tribute which every province used to pay, is replaced by disdain. You yourselves, instead of performing duties of men, follow the path of animals, you have become so effeminate that you have forgotten what a sling or an arrow may be.

'My father the sun has permitted this downfall, and yet has preserved you from falling into slavery. Now his providence will apply a remedy. His command is that you must obey me in all things, as his son. My first decree is that you must apply yourselves to warlike exercises. This you must do, for it was by discipline and exercises that our ancestors became Lords of the World, as our *Quipucamayocs* tell us. Thus occupied, idleness will be driven away, you will become accustomed to obedience, you will recover what has been lost, and you will finally regain the glory that has departed. In my father the sun you will have support. His rays will not dry up the land, nor will the moon deny its rains, evils from which our country has suffered at various times. My laws will be those of the ancient kings, and will not be new inventions. The happy feature of my promises is that they come from my father the sun, and cannot fail. The punishment of disobedience will be thunder that will terrify you, tempests to afflict you, rains to destroy your crops, and lightning to deprive you of life.'

Rocca said all this with such solemnity that no one dared to dispute his words. The whole people proclaimed him their sovereign by acclamation, and the revolution was completed. He began to reign with the title of Inca Rocca. His first act was to remove from the Inti-cancha, which ceased to be the royal residence, and was given up entirely to the temple for the service of the sun. The Inca moved to the upper part of the town, and fixed his residence in an ancient building of the megalithic age. In its wall is the huge stone of twelve corners.

This interesting tradition is told by Montesinos, and is probably near the truth, for there are indications of a revolution of some kind, in Acosta, Morua, and other writers, at the time of Rocca's accession.

An important measure of the new sovereign was the division of people of every district into upper and lower, HANAN and HURIN. Great importance was attached to this arrangement, though it is not quite clear on what grounds it was instituted, and what purposes it was intended to serve. In Cuzco it was decreed that all the descendants of Inca Rocca should be Hanan Cuzcos, and settle in the upper part of the city. Half the *ayllus* which marched to Cuzco with Ayar Manco were also to be Hanan Cuzcos. These were:

    CHAVIN,
    ARAYRACA,
    SAÑOC,
    TARPUNTAY (sacrificer),
    HUACAY TAQUI (sacred music).

Perhaps these five tribes had shown more devotion to the cause of the new ruler than the others. The descendants of Rocca's predecessors were all to be Hurin Cuzcos, and to live in the lower part of the city. The other five original *ayllus* were also Hurin Cuzcos:

    TAMPU (settled at Ollantay-tampu),
    CUYCUSA,
    MASCA (Mascani, I search),
    MARAS (settled at Maras),
    URU (settled at Urupampa).

Probably the division into upper and lower was connected, in some way, with the military exercises which were rigorously enforced by Inca

Rocca. The descendants of the ten original *ayllus* mustered upwards of 20,000 fighting men. Several military expeditions were undertaken, and several neighbouring tribes were subdued—Muyna, Pinahua, Caytomarca, and others—though their territories were not then permanently occupied. But the foundations were laid for a great army, destined to conquer and subjugate the whole Andean region. The ten original *ayllus* were the old guard, round which the rest of the army was formed. The exercises were continuous, and the Inca's son, Vicaquirau, and nephew, Apu Mayta, the two greatest generals the American race has produced, were trained under the eye of the Inca Rocca. It was their prowess and military skill that, during the three following reigns, created the empire of the Incas.

In all respects Inca Rocca appears to have been the pioneer of empire. The last recorded appearance of the lady Siuyacu was when she urged her son to lose no time in suppressing the vicious and slothful habits of the people. He made severe laws with this object, which were rigorously enforced. He also erected schools called *Yachahuasi* to train youths as accountants, and recorders of events. The walls of the Inca's schools still resist the efforts of time. The grand city of later Incas was commenced under the auspices of Rocca. The torrents of Huatanay and Rodadero, rushing down the ravines on either side of the Sacsahuaman hill, had hitherto periodically overflowed their banks, and there were ponds and swamps, one of them on the site of the present cathedral of Cuzco. The Inca Rocca confined the torrents within solid walls, drained the site of the future city, and led off conduits to irrigate the valley. Thus the surrounding country, by a system of terrace cultivation and irrigation, was enabled to support a much larger population.

The custom of boring their ears and enlarging the lobes until they were a great length, which prevailed with the Incas, their relations, and the ten *ayllus*, obtained for them the name of *Hatunrincriyoc*, or great-eared people, which the Spaniards turned into *Orejones*. The latter word is constantly occurring in the early chronicles and narratives, and is a convenient word to use in writing of the Inca nobles. The Incas and their *Orejones*, then, by their greater power and civilisation, and their prestige as children of the sun, had attained to a certain predominance over most of the neighbouring tribes. Yet some stoutly maintained independence, even within a dozen miles of Cuzco, and some, like the Ayamarcas, were hostile and defiant.

CHAPTER VI. THE STOLEN CHILD

A STRANGE and unlooked-for event cast a shadow, though only for a brief period, over the Inca Rocca's life. He had married a very beautiful girl named Micay, the daughter of a neighbouring chief who ruled over a small tribe called PATA HUAYLLACAN. She was the mother of four princes: Cusi Hualpa, the heir, Paucar, Huaman, and Vicaquirau, the future general.

We are told that Micay, the Inca's wife, had previously been promised by her father to Tocay Ccapac, the powerful chief of the Ayamarcas, a much more numerous tribe than the Huayllacans. Her marriage with the Inca caused a deadly feud between those two tribes. Hostilities were continued for a long time, and at last the Huayllacans prayed for peace. It was granted, but with a secret clause that the chief of the Huayllacans would entice away the Inca's eldest son and heir, and deliver him into the hands of his father's enemy, the chief of the Ayamarcas. If this condition was not complied with, Tocay Ccapac declared that he would continue the war until the Huayllacans were blotted out of existence.

These Ayamarcas were at one time a very powerful tribe, in a mountainous region about twenty miles SSW. of Cuzco; while the Huayllacans were in a fertile valley between the Ayamarcas and that city.

In accordance with the agreement, a treacherous plot was laid. An earnest request was sent to the Inca that his heir, the young Cusi Hualpa, might be allowed to visit his mother's relations, so as to become acquainted with them. Quite unsuspicious, the Inca consented and sent the child, who was then about eight years of age, to MICUCANCHA, or PAULU, the chief place of the Huayllacans, with about twenty attendants. The young prince was received with great festivities, which lasted for several days. It was summer time. The sun was scorching, and the child passed his time in a verandah or trellis work, called *arapa*, covered with bright flowers.

One day it was announced that the whole tribe must march to some distance to harvest the crops. As it was still very hot, the Huayllacan chief insisted that the young prince should remain in the shade, and not accompany the harvesters, who had to go a considerable distance under the blazing sun. The prince's attendants consented, and all the tribe, old and young, boys and girls, marched up the hills to the harvesting, singing songs with choruses. All was bright sunshine, and their *haylli*, or harvest song, was in praise of the shade:

> 'Seek the shadow, seek the shade,
> Hide us in the blessed shade.
>> Yahahaha,
>> Yahaha.
>
> 'Where is it? where, where, O where?
> Here it is, here, here, here.
>> Yahahaha,
>> Yahaha.
>
> 'Where the pretty *cantut* blooms,
> Where the *chihua's* flower smiles,
> Where the sweet *amancay* droops.
>> Yahahaha,
>> Yahaha.
>
> 'There it is! there, there, O there!
> Yes, we answer, there, O there.
>> Yahahaha,
>> Yahaha,

The child listened to the sounds of singing as the harvesters passed away out of sight, and then played among the flowers, surrounded by his personal attendants. The place was entirely deserted. When the sound of the singers had died away in the distance there was profound silence. Suddenly, without the slightest warning, the warcry 'Atau!

Atau!' was heard in all directions, and the little party was surrounded by armed men. The Orejones struggled valorously in defence of their precious charge until they were all killed, when the young prince was carried off.

Tocay Ccapac waited to hear the result of his treacherous raid in his chief abode, called Ahuayracancha, or 'the place of woof and warp.' When the raiders returned they entered their chief's presence, with the young prince, shouting 'Behold the prisoner we have brought you.' The chief said, 'Is this the child of Mama Micay, who should have been my wife?' The Prince answered, 'I am the son of the great Inca Rocca and of Mama Micay.' Unsoftened by his tender years, or by his likeness to his beautiful mother, the savage chief ordered the child to be taken out and killed.

Then a strange thing happened. Surrounded by cruel enemies with no pitying eye to look on him, young Cusi Hualpa, a child of eight years, stood up to defy them. He must show himself a child of the sun, and maintain the honour of his race. With a look of indignation beyond his years he uttered a curse upon his captors. His shrill young voice was heard amidst the portentous silence of his enemies. 'I tell you,' he cried, 'that as sure as you murder me there will fall such a curse upon you and your children that you will all come to an end, without any memory being left of your nation.' He ceased, and, to the astonishment of his captors, tears of blood flowed from his eyes. '*Yahuar huaccac!*' '*Yahuar huaccac!*' 'He weeps blood,' they shouted in horror. His curse and this unheard-of phenomenon filled the Ayamarcas with superstitious fear. They recoiled from the murder. Tocay Ccapac and his people thought that the curse from so young a child and the tears of blood betokened some great mystery. They dared not kill him. He stood up in their midst unhurt.

Tocay Ccapac saw that his people would not kill the young prince then, or with their own hands at any time, yet he did not give up his intention of gratifying his thirst for vengeance. He resolved to take the child's life by a course of starvation and exposure. He gave him into the charge of shepherds who tended flocks of llamas on the lofty height overlooking the great plain of Suriti, where the climate is exceedingly rigorous. The shepherds had orders to reduce his food, day by day, until he died.

Young Cusi Hualpa had the gift of making friends. The shepherds did not starve him, though for a year he was exposed to great hardships. No doubt, however, the life he led on those frozen heights improved his health and invigorated his frame.

The Inca was told that his son had mysteriously disappeared, and that his attendants were also missing. The Huayllacan chief expressed sorrow, and pretended that diligent searches had been made. Inca Rocca suspected the Ayamarcas, but did not then attack them, lest, if the child was alive, they might kill him. As time went on the bereaved father began to despair of ever seeing his beloved son again.

Meanwhile the prince was well watched by the shepherds and by a strong guard, which had been sent to ensure his remaining in unknown captivity. But help was at hand. One of the concubines of Tocay Ccapac, named Chimpu Urma, or 'the fallen halo,' had probably been a witness of the impressive scene when the child wept blood. At all events, she was filled with pity and the desire to befriend the forlorn prince. She was a native of Anta, a small town at no great distance from Cuzco. As a friend of Tocay Ccapac she was free to go where she liked, within his dominions and those of the chief of Anta, who was her father.

Chimpu Urma persuaded her relations and friends at Anta to join with her in an attempt to rescue the young prince. It had been arranged by the shepherds and guards that, on a certain day, some boys, including Cusi Hualpa, should have a race up to the top of a hill in front of the shepherds' huts. Hearing this, Chimpu Urma stationed her friends from Anta, well armed, on the other side of the same hill. The race was started, and the prince reached the summit first, where he was taken up in the arms of his Anta friends, who made a rapid retreat. The other boys gave the alarm, and the jailers (shepherds and guards) followed in chase. On the banks of a small lake called Huaylla-punu, the men of Anta, finding that they were being overtaken, made a stand. There was a fierce battle, which resulted in the total defeat of the Ayamarcas. The men of Anta continued their journey, and brought the prince safely to their town, where he was received with great rejoicings.

Cusi Hualpa quite won the hearts of the people of Anta. They could not bear to part with him, and they kept him with great secrecy, delaying to send the joyful news to the Inca. Anta is a small town built up the side of a hill which bounds the vast plain of Suriti to the south. There is a glorious view from it, but the climate is severe. At last, after nearly a year, the Anta people sent messengers to inform the Inca. The child had been given up for lost. All hope had been abandoned. Rocca examined the messengers himself, but still he felt doubt. He feared the news was too good to be true. He secretly sent a man he could trust, as one seeking charity, to Anta, to find out the truth. The Inca's emissary returned with assurances that the young prince was certainly liberated, and was at Anta.

The Inca at last gave way to rejoicing, all doubt being removed. Principal lords were sent with rich presents of gold and silver to the chief of Anta, requesting him to send back the heir to the throne. The chief replied that all his people wished that Cusi Hualpa could remain, for they felt much love for the boy, yet they were bound to restore him to his father. He declined to receive the presents, but he made one condition. It was that he and his people should be accepted as relations of the Inca. So the young prince came back to his parents, and was joyfully received Inca Rocca then visited Anta in person, and declared that the chief and his people were, from henceforward, raised to the rank of Orejones. The Huayllacans made abject submission, and, as Cusi Hualpa generously interceded for them, they were forgiven. Huaman Poma furnishes a curious corroboration of the story of the stolen child. Of all his portraits of the Incas, Rocca is the only one who is portrayed with a little boy. Huaman Poma did not know the story of the kidnapping and the recovered boy—at least, he never mentions it.

All he knew was that only Inca Rocca was to be portrayed with a little boy.

Inca Rocca died after a long and glorious reign, during which he firmly laid the foundations of a great empire. His son Cusi Hualpa succeeded at the age of nineteen. He was commonly known by his surname of YAHUAR HUACCAC, or 'weeping blood.' His reign was memorable for the changes that took place in the system and objects of Inca warfare. The campaigns were no longer mere raids on hostile or rebellious tribes. The Inca's brother, Vicaquirau, and his cousin, Apu Mayta, were administrators quite as much as generals. Every attack on a hostile tribe ended in complete annexation. As the fame of the generals spread, the greater number of tribes submitted without resistance. Those who resisted were made terrible examples of, and if necessary a garrison was left in their principal place. The Ayamarcas were entirely crushed. Thus the Inca realm was every year extended, and at the same time consolidated.

Cusi Hualpa had five sons: Pahuac Hualpa Mayta, so named from his agility as a runner; Hatun Tupac, Vicchu Tupac, Marca Yutu, and Rocca. The Huayllacans, unimpressed by the pardon for their former treachery, conspired to make Marca Yutu the successor of his father, because he was more nearly related to their chief. With this object they enticed Pahuac Hualpa into their power and murdered him. For this there could be no forgiveness, and the tribe was entirely wiped out of existence by the Inca's generals. The second son, Hatun Tupac, then became the heir.

The new heir to the throne had, rather blasphemously, added to his real name of Hatun Tupac, the surname of Uira-cocha, which was that of the Deity. One reason that is given was that, being at Urcos, a town about twenty-five miles south of Cuzco, a vision of the Deity appeared to him in a dream. When he related his experience to his attendants next morning, his tutor, named Hualpa Rimachi, offered congratulations and hailed the young prince as Inca Uira-cocha. Others say that he took the name because he adopted the Deity as his godfather, when he was armed and went through other ceremonies at the festival of Huarachicu. Be this how it may, he always called himself Uira-cocha. His father, mindful of the debt of gratitude he owed to the people of Anta, married his heir to a daughter of their chief, and niece of his deliverer, Chimpu Urma. The lady's name was Runtu-caya.

In the fulness of time Cusi Hualpa (Yahuar Huaccac) was succeeded by his son Hatun Tupac, calling himself Uira-cocha. The policy of the two great generals was continued, and the whole region between the rivers Apurimac and Vilcamayu, the Inca region, was annexed and consolidated into one realm under the Inca. The names of Uira-cocha's sons by Runtu-caya were Rocca, Tupac, and Cusi. By a beautiful concubine named Ccuri-chulpa the Inca had two other sons named Urco and Sucso. For the sake of Ccuri-chulpa he favoured her children, and even declared the bastard Urco to be his heir. His eldest son was a valiant young warrior, trained in the school of Vicaquirau and Apu Mayta, and, when his age was sufficient, this prince Rocca became their colleague. Cusi was the most promising youth of the rising generation, endowed with rare gifts, beautiful in form and feature, of dauntless courage and universally beloved.

CHAPTER VII. EMPIRE

THE land of the Incas! the land of the sovereign city! the land of the sacred vale! The land converted from the home of many contending tribes, to a realm obedient to one king and lord. This change had been due to the great military skill and administrative ability of the two generals, Apu Mayta and Vicaquirau. It was a work of many years, but it was completed.

The land of the Incas was 250 miles in length by 60 in width. It is bounded on its western side by the river Apurimac, 'chief of the speaking waters,' dashing down a profound ravine with precipitous sides. On the east was the Vilcamayu, 'the sacred river,' flowing from the 'sacred lake' (*Vilca uñuta*) at the foot of the lofty snowy peak which is visible from Cuzco, rising majestically into the azure sky. Unlike the Apurimac, the Vilcamayu irrigates a wide and fertile valley unsurpassed for beauty in the wide world. To the south this classic land is separated from the basin of Lake Titicaca by the knot of Vilcañota, which connects the eastern and maritime Cordilleras. To the north the wild mountains of Vilcapampa finally sink down into the tropical Amazonian forests.

Between the rivers there are four zones, in which the aspects of the land differ, mainly owing to varying elevations above the sea. To the south there is a vast extent of lofty tableland, with a very rigorous climate, where there were flocks of llamas, some scattered villages, and a few large lakes. Next, to the north, is the region of mountains and valleys with drainage to the two rivers. This was the most densely inhabited zone, yielding crops of maize and of edible roots. In its centre is Cuzco, with its two torrents of Huatanay and Tulumayu, uniting and then flowing down its long valley to join the sacred river. There were other valleys with picturesque lakes, and ravines filled with trees and flowering bushes. The lakes were frequented by a large goose (*huallata*), two ducks (*nuñuma* and *huachua*), flamingoes, cranes, herons, egrets, and a black ibis, as well as the Andean gull (*quellua*). The sides of the hills were occupied by terraced cultivation, but above the terraces the slopes were frequented by partridges (*yutu*) and quails (*chuy*), plover (*llecco-llecco*) and the Andean hare or *uiscacha*. Sometimes a condor might be made out, far up in the sky, like a black speck, while eagles (*anca*) and falcons (*alcamari* and *huaman*) are occasionally seen, soaring in mid air. Other birds, at these great elevations, are the *chihua*, a sort of thrush, the *chanquiri* or crow, and a few of the finch tribe.

In this country of lakes and well-watered ravines was the Tamputocco district, on the Apurimac side, whence the Ayar Manco marched to Cuzco. Here, too, were the territories of the Muynas, Pinahuas, Huayllacans, Canchis, Caviñas, Ayamarcas, and other tribes. The great elevation only admitted of a somewhat lowly flora. Yet it is the native place of the graceful *Schinus molli*-tree, with its pinnate leaves and bunches of red berries. With it there are several large flowering bushes called *chilca*, compositse belonging to *Baccharis Molina* and *Eupatorium*, and *tasta* (*Stereoxylon patens*). Higher up are the *queñua*, *ccolli*, and *quisuar* trees, and the *tola* bush already described. There are ferns too, and many wild flowers. Chief among them ranked the golden lily (*Amaryllis aurea*) and a red liliaceous flower. The *cantut* was a bright-coloured phlox, much used for garlands. The meadows and ravines were also enlivened by salvias, valerians, calceolarias, lupins, some large yellow compositae, a convolvulus, a tropoeolum, and many herbs used medicinally.

Above these pleasant valleys, and on either side of Cuzco, are two lofty plateaux, desolate and frequented only by shepherds and their flocks. Between the city and the Vilcamayu valley is the highland of Chita. On the Apurimac side is the wild region whither the kidnapped prince was sent by the chief of Ayamarca. The third zone, further north, comprises the vast plain of Suriti or Ychupampa, and the plateau overlooking the sacred valley. From the crest of the Apurimac gorge the road leads up over the two pleasant valleys of Mollepata and Rimac-tampu, and then by a slight ascent to the great plain covered with grass and reeds, where there are occasionally swamps and morasses. This plain is surrounded by mountains; on their slopes are picturesque little towns, such as Suriti and Anta, and at its south-eastern end a ravine leads down, by Iscuchaca, to the city of Cuzco, about twelve miles distant. There are swamps, but there are also vast tracts of *ychu* or coarse grass, where the llama flocks of Anta find pasture. Towards the end of winter storms of thunder and lightning, with rain, pass rapidly over the plain. It is an indescribably grand sight to see these storms drifting across, with the sun shining behind them, and causing exquisite effects of light and shade, while snowy egrets and darker curlew whirl in circles over the swamps.

East of the Suriti plain, which is an ideal battlefield, there is a plateau overlooking the Vilcamayu valley. Here are the small towns of Maras and Chinchero, with cultivated patches round them, on the verge of the descent.

But the gem of the land of the Incas is the sacred valley, the 'valley' *par excellence*, as it was called. Rising in the sacred lake at the foot of the snowy peak of Vilcañota, the valley of Vilcamayu increases in fertility and beauty as the river descends. The most lovely part is from Pissac to Ollantay-tampu, where the mighty Andes sends up its snowy peaks on one side, and precipitous cliffs bound the other. The groves of fine trees are alive with singing-birds—the *checollo*, with a song like our nightingale, the pretty *tuyas* and *chaynas*, the bright-plumaged *ccamantira* and *choccla-poccochi*, and the *ccenti*, or humming-bird. Here, too, are doves and pigeons, the *urpi* and *cullcu*, and the golden-breasted *quitu*. There are also many small green paroquets. In the valley are raised splendid crops of maize, unequalled elsewhere, grown on terraces arranged in patterns, and the fruit gardens are filled with *chirimoya*, *palta*, *lucuma*, and *paccay* trees, up which twine the passion flowers with their refreshing fruit. In this enchanting valley the Incas had their most delightful country palace of Yucay, with extensive baths and gardens. The wide world might be searched without finding a rival, in enchanting beauty, to the sacred valley of the Incas.

The most northern zone is occupied by the wild mountainous district of Vilcapampa, between the two rivers, here forty miles apart.

This land of the Incas had been brought under a settled government, and there was a breathing time of peace. But intrigue and discontent were rife in Cuzco. Uira-cocha Inca, who was old and wholly under the influence of his concubine Ccuri-chulpa, had passed over all his legitimate sons, and declared the bastard Urco to be his heir. The two veteran generals, Apu Mayta and Vicaquirau, and the legitimate sons, were resolved that this should not be. There was internal trouble ahead, but much greater danger threatened from without. While the Incas were consolidating their rule between the two rivers, the heads of other confederacies were doing the same elsewhere. The most formidable confederacy was that of the Chancas. The founders of this powerful kingdom were two chiefs named Uscovilca and Ancovilca. They established their principal seat in the extensive and fertile valley of Andahuaylas, and their descendants had conquered the greater part of the western and northern districts of the Andes. The Chanca chiefs were warlike and ambitious, and they had a great military force at their command.

The chiefs of the Chancas were two brothers named Asto-huaraca and Tomay-huaraca, proud and insolent warriors who could not endure the existence of any neighbours who maintained their independence. The river Apurimac separated their territory from that of the children of the sun, and they resolved to bring the Inca under subjection. They sent a messenger to Cuzco demanding submission, and, without waiting for an answer, they crossed the Apurimac with a numerous army, advancing over the great plain of Suriti or Ychupampa. In their wars the Chancas carried an image of their founder, Uscovilca, in front of the army, because it had hitherto always led them to victory. They called it ANCO AYLLU.

The news of the rapid approach of this formidable army spread consternation in Cuzco, in the midst of the intrigues about the succession of Urco. The old Inca had not the courage to face the enemy, and resolved upon flight to a strongly fortified position, called Caquia Saquis-ahuana, overlooking Pissac in the valley. His way took him over the highlands of Chita. His illegitimate sons, Urco and Sucso, fled with him, and a great following of Orejones and their families. Cuzco was deserted and left to its fate. The Inca encamped on the plateau of Chita to await events, before finally shutting himself up in Caquia Saquis-ahuana. He had hopes from negotiation with the Chancas.

The two old generals and the legitimate sons refused to leave Cuzco. They declared that they would die in defence of their homes, and of the gods of their people. Three other chiefs remained with them, but all the force they could collect consisted of little more than their own personal followers.

Who was to command this forlorn hope? There was not a day to lose. The enemy was almost at the gates. The generals declared for the youngest of the Inca's sons, Prince Cusi, who had just reached his twentieth year. He was a child of destiny. Rocca had laid the foundations. Cusi was the builder of the empire. It was a remarkable testimony to his genius that, not only the old generals, but his elder brothers accepted him as their leader and remained faithful to him to the end. His seven chiefs were enthusiastic, but that was not enough. The odds were terrible, apparently hopeless. Seven leaders and perhaps 700 followers, not more, rallied round the young prince:

1. *Vicaquirau*, his great-uncle;
2. *Apu Mayta*, his first cousin twice removed; generals, and heroes of a hundred battles.
3. *Rocca*, his eldest brother;
4. *Paucar*, his next eldest brother; able and experienced officers.
5. *Urco Huaranca*, chief of *Quilliscancha* (a Cuzco suburb).
6. *Chima Chaui Pata*.
7. *Mircay-maña*, tutor to Prince Cusi.

Cusi first saw that every man was well armed, and trained, and in high spirits. He did not conceal the odds from them, yet he assured the little band of heroes that the Deity was on their side. He sent out summonses to all the vassals, but with little or no success. He exhorted the few who remained in the suburbs to defend their homes. He went especially to the Quilliscancha suburb accompanied by its brave chief, Urco Huaranca. Here there was some enthusiasm, and it was clear that he would find support. Moreover, arrangements were made to obtain information through a Quilliscancha scout. The armed leader of the suburb was a valiant and stalwart lady named Chañan-ccuri-coca, on whose loyalty the prince placed reliance. Having made all the preparations that were possible with the small means at his command, Cusi retired to a lonely place to pray to his god. There is a fountain called the SUSUR PUQUIO, between Iscuchaca and Cuzco, a secluded spot where a stream, shaded by molle trees, falls over some rocks. Here Prince Cusi knelt in prayer. He had a vision. A figure, resplendent and dazzling, appeared to him in the air, which he knew to be his father the sun. He was consoled and animated for the battle, with the assurance that he would conquer the Chancas. The prince returned to his followers, and imparted to them the enthusiasm by which he was himself inspired. A number of vassals came from a distance, but more inclined to look on than to fight. They took to the hills to watch the event.

The Chancas advanced in great numbers, full of confidence, without order, and expecting little or no resistance. One of the scouts sent by Urco Huaranca rushed into the prince's presence crying, 'To arms! To arms! The foe is upon us.' The Chancas were entering Cuzco, but met with a stubborn resistance in the Quilliscancha suburb. Prince Cusi was ready, and all his plans were laid. Followed closely by the aged generals, his elder brothers, and their followers, in a compact phalanx, he made a sudden and furious flank attack, forcing his way in like a wedge, and making straight for the statue and standard of Uscovilca. While a furious battle was raging in the suburb, Asto-huaraca and

Tomayhuaraca rallied their guards to defend their standard. But the flank attack was so furious and so well sustained, that the Chancas were amazed and thrown into confusion. Prince Cusi was so dexterous with his weapon that no one could resist him, and he hewed his way straight for the standard. He was ably sustained by his followers, and there was great havoc. The Chanca chiefs lost heart and ordered a retreat.

When the crowds of recreant vassals on the hills saw this, they came down to join the little Inca force, converting the retreat into a rout. This explains the story, told by several writers, that the sun made armed men rise out of the earth to complete the victory. The Chanca standard and the spoils of their camp were captured.

The greatness of this victory, which saved the Inca realm from complete destruction, was as astonishing as it was unexpected. Prince Cusi was hailed as the Inca Pachacuti, the ninth bearing that title, counting those of the old dynasties. Henceforward he was known by no other name. He refused to allow a triumphal ceremony for himself, but sent Urco Huaranca with all the spoils to his father at the camp on the Chita highlands, that he might tread upon them, according to the usual custom. Uira-cocha refused to do this himself, but delegated the duty to his son Urco, as the heir to the kingdom. Urco Huaranca was furious, declaring that no coward should triumph by the deeds of Pachacuti, and returning with the spoils to Cuzco.

We hear no more of the great generals, Vicaquirau and Apu Mayta. They either found a glorious death on the battlefield or died soon afterwards at a great age. Pachacuti's eldest brother, Rocca, was his most trusted general. There was no longer any difficulty about raising troops, and an efficient army was organised, well drilled and armed with slings, arrows, axes, and clubs. For the Chancas, though repulsed, were by no means crushed. They retired to the great plain of Ychupampa, received large reinforcements from the other side of the Apurimac, and prepared for another march upon Cuzco. But now the Inca Pachacuti was strong enough to take the initiative, and he made such a rapid march that he found the Chanca army still encamped on the great plain. The hostile chiefs, encouraged by the arrival of large reinforcements, had regained much of their confidence. Their army was as numerous as before the defeat, their principal weapons being long lances. When the chiefs saw the approach of the Inca army, they sent an insolent message threatening to dye their lances with the Inca's blood if he did not at once submit and become a tributary vassal. Pachacuti calmly replied that no more time could be wasted in talk, and that God would give the victory to whom he pleased. He marched onwards with his army, following closely on the heels of the messenger.

The contending forces closed in deadly hand-to-hand combat, and the battle raged for a long time without advantage on either side. At last Pachacuti, with his immediate guards, hewed his way through the hostile ranks to where Asto-huaraca was fighting. There was a duel, and the Chanca chief was slain. His colleague, Tomay-huaraca, was already killed. The Inca ordered the heads of the two chiefs to be raised up on their own lances. This caused a panic, and the hostile army broke and fled. The Orejones followed in pursuit, doing great execution, few escaping over the terrific gorge of the Apurimac in their rear.

The power of the great confederacy was completely broken. It was a death struggle. For a long time the balance seemed to incline to the Chancas. The valour and genius of Cusi, the Pachacuti, turned the scale, and the empire of the Incas was the result. The tributary vassals of the Chancas, over a vast area, soon changed their allegiance, some after slight resistance, but the greater number voluntarily and with good will.

Pachacuti went in person to his father, who had now taken refuge in his stronghold called Caquia Saquis-ahuana, with the prisoners and spoils, requesting the old man to tread upon them according to custom. He still desired that his favourite son Urco should perform the ceremony, but was at last persuaded to comply with the custom himself. It was called *Muchanacu*.

On his return to Cuzco there was a solemn sacrifice to the sun, and the Inca Pachacuti was crowned with the fringe, and proclaimed sole lord and sovereign in the lifetime of his father. Most of the Orejones who had fled with Uira-cocha returned to Cuzco. Soon after his accession the news reached Pachacuti that Urco had assembled forces in the valley, whether with or without the connivance of his father is uncertain. The Inca, with his brother Rocca, at once marched against the insurgents. Urco received a blow on the neck from a stone hurled by his brother Rocca. He fell into the river and was carried down to a rock called Chupillusca, a league below Ollantay-tampu, where he tried to land, but was killed by his brothers. They then sought an interview with their father, who refused to see the Inca, but Rocca forced his way into the old man's presence and upbraided him. Uira-cocha continued to live in his stronghold of Caquia Saquis-ahuana, where he died and was buried. In his prime he loved gorgeous display, and we are told that he was the inventor of a kind of rich cloth or brocade called TOCAPU. The name of his stronghold may have reference to this, for AHUANA means a loom. CAQUIA may be rendered 'my possession' or 'property.'

The Prince Cusi was the builder of the empire, the foundations of which were laid by Rocca. The elaborate religious ceremonial, the methods of recording events, the military organisation, the self-working social system were his work. It may seem incredible that the whole fabric of Andean civilisation should be the work of one man, and it would be if he had created it. But Cusi was not the creator. He was the PACHACUTI, the reformer. Over all the regions that he conquered there were the same ideas and habits of thought, and of living, dialects of the same original language, and the same faint memories of an almost forgotten past. Pachacuti worked upon these materials with the skill and foresight of a profound statesman. His grand object was attained, for he welded together a homogeneous empire with such masterly thoroughness in all its complicated details that its machinery worked almost automatically.

Pachacuti was a great conqueror as well as a great administrator. The immediate consequence of the final victory over the Chancas and of the disruption of their confederacy was the addition of a vast territory to the land of the Incas. The country beyond the Apurimac, between that river and the Pachachaca, submitted at once. It was the land of the Quichuas, very closely allied to the Incas. The next region, between the river Pachachaca and the Pampas, containing the beautiful valley of Andahuaylas, the chief seat of the Chancas, also submitted. The Chancas even added an important contingent to the Inca army. Beyond the Pampas, the Soras and Lucanas, hardy mountaineers, submitted after a brief struggle. These were the first fruits of the victory over the Chancas. Pachacuti next invaded the basin of Lake Titicaca, and the whole region was annexed after three hard-fought campaigns against the Collas.

Then followed a campaign during which the whole northern region of the Andes, as far as Caxamarca, was added to the empire.

By this time Pachacuti was well stricken in years. His eldest son was Amaru Tupac, a very able and successful general, who was, at one time, intended to be his heir. But the question of the succession was a very important one, and something more was needed than a successful general. By his wife Anahuarqui, the Inca had another son, also named Tupac, in whom the great statesman saw the germs of such genius as would fit him to succeed to the responsibility of guiding an empire. After an interview with his father, the eldest son, Amaru, accepted the situation and remained loyal to his younger brother until death. Young Tupac went through the ceremony of being armed, and then proceeded on a great northern campaign. The countries of Huamanca, Jauja, Huanucu, Caxamarca, and Chachapoyas were united to the empire, as well as the coast valleys. Young Tupac also subdued the Cañaris, and extended his conquests to Quito. He then descended to the coast, annexing the country of Manta, with its emeralds, and even making a successful voyage over the Pacific Ocean to the Galapagos Islands.

The end of the great emperor came at last, after a memorable reign of more than half a century. He bad his sons and his councillors around him. Addressing Tupac, he said: 'My son, you know how many great nations I leave to you, and you know what labour they have cost me. Mind that you are the man to keep and augment them.' He made his other sons plough furrows and he gave them weapons, in token that they were to serve and to fight for their sovereign. He turned to Tupac saying, 'Care for them, and they will serve you.' He expressed some wishes about his obsequies, ordering that his body should be placed in his palace of Pata-llacta. Then he began to croon in a low and sad voice:

> 'I was born as a flower of the field,
> As a flower I was cherished in my youth,
> I came to my full age, I grew old;
> Now I am withered and die.'

He told those around him that he went to rest with his father the sun—and so he departed, the greatest man that the American race has ever produced.

Tupac was a worthy successor. He continued and consolidated the work of his father. As his power and the extent of the empire increased, the Incas assumed greater state and magnificence. With Pachacuti apparently, and certainly with Tupac, the custom of marrying sisters was commenced. Like the Ptolemies, the Incas resorted to this method of making their family a race apart from the rest of mankind and almost divine.

Tupac was second only to his father as an administrator and a general. His first campaign as a sovereign was a most difficult one. He penetrated far into the primeval forests to the east of the Andes. He then completely subjugated the Collas, and Chile as far as the river Maule. His long reign extended over upwards of sixty years, mainly a period of consolidation. He established a firm and settled government on the lines laid down by his father. When he felt the approach of death, he retired to his palace of Chinchero, overlooking the sacred valley, with a glorious view of the snowy mountains. The walls of this palace are still standing. The dying Inca sent for his relations and councillors, and announced to them that his heir and successor was to be the young Prince Cusi Hualpa, his legitimate son by his sister and wife, Mama Ocllo. He then sank down among his pillows and died at the great age of eighty-five years.

Cusi Hualpa was then with his tutors at Quispicancha, in the valley. He was brought to Cuzco, and invested with all the insignia of royalty; and his accession was announced to the people in the Rimac-pampa, an open space near the temple of the sun. Surprised at the youthful appearance of their sovereign, their acclamations were mingled with cries of 'Huayna! Huayna!' (the boy-king, the boy-king). From thenceforward his surname was Huayna Ccapac. After a few years of administration at Cuzco, the young Inca made a visitation of all his dominions from Chile to Quito. The last part of his reign was occupied with a very ably conducted campaign on the extreme northern borders of his empire, and he died at Quito in 1525, the last of the great imperial Incas, great in peace as in war.

The six Incas, from Rocca to Huayna, may, with fair probability, be given a period of 300 years; and the Ayar Manco's date would be about 1100 A.D.

CHAPTER VIII. RELIGION OF THE INCAS

IT is very difficult to obtain a correct and clear idea of the religious beliefs of a people like the Peruvians, whose thoughts and traditions were entirely different from those of the nations of the old world. Besides the inherent difficulty of comprehending the bent of their minds, which resulted in the religious practices recorded of them, there are many others. The record was made by very superstitious priests, with strong prejudices against the beliefs of the conquered people, and with only a general knowledge of the language. There was but one important authority who had known the language from childhood. The manuscripts were often incorrectly transcribed by ignorant clerks, so that mistakes and misspellings crept into the texts, and there were contradictions among the authorities. On the whole it is fortunate that there should have been such painstaking and conscientious writers as Blas Valera, Cieza de Leon, and Molina, upon whose evidence reliance can be placed as, at all events, the impartial impressions of the writers. Still, a very careful weighing of the amount of trust to be given to the various authorities is necessary, with reference to their characters, positions, and circumstances; as well as a comparison of the same statement in various authorities, in order to judge which version is nearest to the truth, and to arrive at the nearest approximation to accuracy. Such a scrutiny is the work of years, but the subject, from every point of view, is worthy of this serious and prolonged study.

The god who was regarded as the creator and ruler of the universe in the megalithic age was, as we have seen, ILLA TICI UIRA-COCHA. The names were handed down, by tradition, through the centuries, and were used by the Incas when contemplating or worshipping the Supreme Being. The names came to them, and were not invented by them. For them they were the names of the ruler of the universe, whatever their meaning might be. For the Incas, and the more thoughtful among those who surrounded them, were convinced that the deities worshipped by the people were not supreme, but that they obeyed some irresistible and unknown but orderly force. It was this Supreme Being that the Incas worshipped, and sought, with fervency, to know and to understand. Both Molina and Salcamayhua tell us that there was a temple at Cuzco to the Supreme Being, and that his worship was included in the elaborate ritual of the later Incas. Molina gives the prayers that were offered to Uira-cocha, whose temple is stated to have been apart from the temple of the sun. Salcamayhua tells us that the Supreme Creator was represented in the sun temple by an oval slab of gold, having a higher place than the images of the sun or moon. The prayers were for health and strength, for good harvests and the multiplication of flocks, for victory over enemies, and for prosperity. Nine of these prayers, in Quichua, are given by Molina. One is given by Morua. The most remarkable prayer is that for the sun, called PUNCHAU, in which it is fully recognised that its movements and heat-attributes are the work of Uira-cocha.

This recognition of an almighty, unseen being who created and regulates all things visible was probably confined to the higher intellects, who had more time and were better trained for thought and reflection. The rest of the people would seek for visible objects of worship. But for the Incas the Uira-cocha cult was certainly very real. It occupied their thoughts in life and in death, and they earnestly prayed for a knowledge of the Deity. Some of the hymns addressed to the Almighty have been preserved in a manuscript written early in the seventeenth century by a native named Yamqui Pachacuti Salcamayhua. They were first printed by the present writer in a translation of Salcamayhua's work (1873), the text of the hymns being left in the original Quichua. Some years afterwards the Spanish text was edited by Don Marcos Jimenez de la Espada at Madrid, but again without any attempt to translate the Quichua hymns. This was at last done through the instrumentality of Don Samuel A. Lafone Quevedo. The text was very corrupt, the words were misspelt and not divided from each other, and it would require a most profound Quichua scholar to restore the meaning of the original. Señor Lafone Quevedo secured the services of Dr. Miguel Mossi, of Bolivia, now no more, by far the best modern scholar of the language of the Incas. The result was the publication in 1892 of Spanish translations of the hymns to Uira-cocha. These hymns are the expression of a longing to know the invisible god, to walk in his ways, and to have the prayers heard which entreat the Deity to reveal himself. They show a strong sense of his guiding power in regulating the seasons and the courses of the heavenly bodies, and in making provision for reproduction in nature. There is a strange expression of wonder respecting the sex of the Deity; but this is wonder and nothing more, not, as Señor Lafone Quevedo suggests, an allusion to phallic worship. There is, indeed, a plaintive note in these cries to the Deity for a knowledge of the unknowable, which is touching in its simplicity.

> O Uira-cocha! Lord of the universe,
> Whether thou art male,
> Whether thou art female,
> Lord of reproduction,
> Whatsoever thou mayest be,
> O Lord of divination,
> Where art thou?
> Thou mayest be above,
> Thou mayest be below,
> Or perhaps around
> Thy splendid throne and sceptre.
> Oh hear me!
> From the sky above,
> In which thou mayest be,
> From the sea beneath,
> In which thou mayest be,
> Creator of the world,
> Maker of all men;
> Lord of all Lords,
> My eyes fail me
> For longing to see thee;
> For the sole desire to know thee.

>
> Might I behold thee,
> Might I know thee,
> Might I consider thee,
> Might I understand thee.
> Oh look down upon me,
> For thou knowest me.
> The sun—the moon—
> The day—the night—
> Spring—winter,
> Are not ordained in vain
> By thee, O Uira-cocha!
> They all travel
> To the assigned place;
> They all arrive
> At their destined ends,
> Whithersoever thou pleasest.
> Thy royal sceptre
> Thou holdest.
> Oh hear me!
> Oh choose me!
> Let it not be
> That I should tire,
> That I should die.

One of the hymns is composed as from an aged Inca on his death-bed praying for light and for a knowledge of the Deity.

> O creator of men,
> Thy servant speaks,
> Then look upon him,
> Oh, have remembrance of him,
> The King of Cuzco.
> I revere you, too, Tarapaca.
> O Tonapa, look down,
> Do not forget me.
> O thou noble Creator,
> O thou of my dreams,
> Dost thou already forget,
> And I on the point of death?
> Wilt thou ignore my prayer,

> Or wilt thou make known
> Who thou art?
> Thou mayst be what I thought,
> Yet perchance thou art a phantom,
> A thing that causes fear.
> Oh, if I might know!
> Oh, if it could be revealed!
> Thou who made me out of earth,
> And of clay formed me,
> Oh look upon me!
> Who art thou, Creator,
> Now I am very old.

Another hymn to Uira-cocha is attributed, by Salcamayhua, to the Inca Rocca:

> Oh come then,
> Great as the heavens,
> Lord of all the earth,
> Great First Cause,
> Creator of men.
> Ten times I adore thee,
> Ever with my eyes
> Turned to the ground,
> Hidden by the eyelashes,
> Thee am I seeking.
> Oh look on me!
> Like as for the rivers,
> Like as for the fountains,
> When gasping with thirst,
> I seek for thee.
> Encourage me,
> Help me!
> With all my voice
> I call on thee;
> Thinking of thee,
> We will rejoice
> And be glad.
> This will we say
> And no more.

These fragments, broken chips from a great wreck, have at last reached us. We know from them that, in their inmost hearts, the intellectual and more instructed section of the Incas and their people sought for a knowledge of the unseen creator of the universe, while publicly conducting the worship of objects which they knew to be merely God's creatures. Garcilasso de la Vega gives the sayings of several Incas respecting the obedience of the sun, in its daily and yearly course, to the behests of a higher power. There are one or two points connected with Uira-cocha which have been puzzling, and which will be better discussed in a footnote.

The cult of Uira-cocha by the Incas was confined to the few. The popular religion of the people was the worship of the founder or first ancestor of each *ayllu* or clan. The father of the Incas was the sun, and naturally all the people joined in the special adoration of the ancestor of their sovereign, combined with secondary worship of the moon, thunder and lightning, the rainbow, and the dawn, represented by the morning star CHASCA. But each clan or *ayllu* had also a special huaca, or ancestral god, which its members worshipped in common, besides the household gods of each family.

In the last century or two, the ceremonial and ritual observances of the sun-worship at Cuzco assumed extraordinary magnificence. The splendid temple was built of masonry, which, for the beauty and symmetry of its proportions and the accuracy with which the stones fitted into each other, is unsurpassed. The cornices, the images, and the utensils were all of pure gold. When the Inca and his court were present at the ceremonies it must have been a scene of marvellous splendour.

The elaborate ritual and ceremonies necessitated the employment of a numerous hierarchy, divided into many grades. The High Priest was an official of the highest rank, often a brother of the sovereign. He was called *Uillac Uma*, 'the head which counsels.' He was the supreme judge and arbiter in all religious questions and causes relating to the temples. His life was required to be passed in religious contemplation and abstinence. He was a strict vegetarian and never drank anything but water. His ordinary dress was a robe going down to the ankles, and a grey mantle of vicuña wool. But when he celebrated the festivals in the temple he wore the grand tiara, called *Uilca Chucu*, which included a circular plate of gold representing the sun, and under the chin a half-moon of silver. The head-dress was adorned with the feathers of the *guacamaya*, or great macaw; the whole covered with jewels and plates of gold. The complete head-dress was called *Huampar Chucu*. His ceremonial tunic without sleeves reached to the ground, with no belt. Over it there was a shorter pelisse of white wool, trimmed with red, which came down to the knees, and was covered with precious stones and plates of gold. His shoes were of fine wool, and bracelets of gold were on his arms. Directly the ceremony was over he divested himself of his vestments and remained in his ordinary clothes. He received ample rents, bestowing the greater part on those afflicted by blindness or other disabling infirmities. Besides being of illustrious lineage, the High Priest was an *Amauta*, or man of learning. He appointed the visitors and inspectors whose duty it was to report on all the temples and idols throughout the empire; and the confessors (*Ichuri*) who received confessions and assigned penances; and he superintended the record of events by the *Amautas* and *Quipucamayocs*. On his death the body was embalmed and interred with great pomp on some high mountain.

Under the *Uillac Uma* there were ten or twelve chief priests in the provinces, called *Uilca*, who had authority over the very numerous priests in charge of *huacas*, called *Huacap Uillac*, and over those who received and announced oracles from the *huacas, Huacap Rimachi*.

A very remarkable and interesting institution was that of the chosen virgins for the service of the sun, called *Aclla*. They were also known as *Intip Chinan*, or *Punchau Chinan*, servants of the sun; selected by inspectors from all parts of the empire. All the sun temples had virgins, those at Cuzco coming chiefly from the neighbourhood of the city, from Huanuco and Chachapoyas. After examination they were placed under the government of matrons, called *Mama Cuna*, and had to serve a novitiate. There were over 3000 virgins at Cuzco, with a matron for every ten. Each virgin had a servant. The novitiate lasted for three years, during which time the girls were taught to sew, weave, make fine bread and cakes, sweep and clean the temple, and keep alive the sacred fire which was always burning, called *Nina Uilca*. Many princesses and daughters of nobles were sent to be educated with the novices, although they were not going to be *Aclla*. When the novices had served their three years they were called *Huamac*. They were brought before the Inca and the *Uillac Uma*. Those who did not feel a vocation received husbands. Those who wished to remain as virgins of the sun were dressed in white, and garlands of gold (*Ccuri Uincha*) were placed on their heads. They were dedicated to the sun for the rest of their lives, employed in the service of the temple, and in weaving very fine cloth for the deities, the Inca and his family, and the *Uillac Uma*. They never went abroad without an armed escort, and were treated with profound respect. When the Spanish destruction came, many of these virgins became nuns and were protected, others married baptised Indians, and the rest fled in various directions.

Another numerous class in this complicated hierarchy was that of diviners and soothsayers, called *Huatuc*. They were dressed in grey, were celibate while holding office, living on herbs and roots, and were almost always to be found in the vestibules of the temples. Those who divined by the flight of birds and by the intestines of animals sacrificed were called *Hamurpa*. The *Lllaychunca* divined by odds and evens, the *Pacchacuc* by the legs of a great hairy spider, the *Socyac* by maize heaps, the *Hualla, Achacuc, Canchu, Canahuisa, Layca,* and *Yarcacaes* in other ways. The *Macsa* cured by enchantment.

There was an elaborate system of sacrifices, entailing an enormous expenditure. The victims were llamas, huanacus, vicuñas and their lambs, pumas, antas or tapirs, birds and their plumes, maize, edible roots, coca, shells, cloth, gold, silver, sweet woods, guinea-pigs, dogs, in short everything they valued. The sacrificing priest was called *Tarpuntay*; the lay brother who cut up the victims, *Nacac*; and the recorder, *Uilca Camayoc*. The sacrifice itself was called *Arpay*. There remains the question of human sacrifices, or *Ccapac Cocha*. The idea of sacrifice is the offering of what is most prized. The sacrificer says to his god: 'What I loved best to thee I gave.'

Abraham was ready to sacrifice his son, the king of Moab actually did so. It is the logical outcome of sacrificial doctrine. Was this logical conclusion reached by the Peruvians, either habitually or in extreme cases? The weight of evidence is certainly against the accusation, which was first made by the licentiate Polo de Ondegardo in 1554, when he was conducting inquiries at Cuzco. He says that grown men and children were sacrificed on various occasions, and that 200 boys were sacrificed at the accession of Huayna Ccapac. Valera denies the value of Polo's evidence, who, he says, scarcely knew anything of the language, had no interpreters at that time, and was without the means of becoming acquainted with the ancient customs. So that he could not fail to write down many things which were quite different from what the Indians said. Polo was followed by Molina and others, especially by Sarmiento, whose official instructions were to make the worst of the Inca polity and government.

Valera declares, on the contrary, that there was a law prohibiting all sacrifices of human beings, which was strictly observed. It is true that *Huahuas*, or children, and *Yuyacs*, or adults, were sacrificed, but the *Huahuas* were lambs, not human children, and by *Yuyac* were meant full-grown llamas, not men. Valera is supported by Garcilasso de la Vega and other authorities, and the weight of evidence is decidedly against Polo's accusation.

There remains the logical tendency of the sacrificial idea to offer up the dearest and most valued possession; while the admission of Blas Valera that there was a law against human sacrifices seems to show that they were not unknown. Cieza de Leon is the most unprejudiced and the most reliable of all the authorities, and he says that if human sacrifices were ever offered, they were of very rare occurrence. This is probably the truth. The horrible offerings were not common nor habitual, but they had been known to be offered, on very extreme and exceptional occasions.

With the worship of the ancestor, *Paccarisca*, or the fabulous origin of each clan, whether the sun, the moon, a star, a mountain, rock, spring, or any other natural object, the Peruvians had some peculiar beliefs which pervaded their daily life. They had special personal deities in which they trusted. The sovereign Incas kept such images always with them and gave them names, calling them *Huauqui*, or brother. That of the Inca Uira-cocha was called *Inca Amaru*, probably in the form of a serpent. It was found by Polo de Ondegardo, with that Inca's ashes. Pachacuti had a very large golden *Huauqui*, called *Inti Illapa*, which was sent in pieces to Caxamarca for the ransom. *Cusi Churi* was the name of the *Huauqui* of the Inca Tupac, which was found concealed at Calis Puquio, near Cuzco, by Polo. The *Huauqui* of Huayna Ccapac, a gold image of great value, has never been found. It was called *Huaraqui Inca*. The tradition handed down in the Incarial family is that the *Huauqui* of Manco Ccapac was a sacred bird called *Inti*, kept in a sort of hamper; that of Sinchi Rocca was called *Huanachici Amaru*; that of Lloque Yupanqui, *Apu Mayta*. The rest of the Orejones and many others had their special *Lar* or brother, and the *Huauqui* was buried with the body of the deceased.

The universal belief of the Peruvians was that all things in nature had a spiritual essence or counterpart, to which prayers and sacrifice might be offered if the spirit belonged to any of the reproductive powers of nature, or good might be done to it, if the departed spirit was a relation or friend. This explains the method of interment and the rites and ceremonies observed for the wellbeing of the departed. It was thought that so long as the embalmed body was carefully preserved, with the personalty of the deceased, the welfare of the departed spirit was secured. So long as food and other requisites were duly placed with the mummy, the spirit would be furnished with the spiritual essence of all that was offered materially. These strange beliefs occupied the thoughts and pervaded the lives of the people.

The funeral ceremonies of the Incas were occasions for all the magnificence and pomp of a great empire. The body was embalmed and splendidly attired. The palace of the deceased was set apart for the *Malqui*, or mummy, a staff of servants was appointed for it, and it was endowed with lands, so that offerings might be constantly provided. Friends and dependants were invited to immolate themselves so as to accompany their lord in the spirit world, but in later times a llama was allowed as a substitute, the name of the supposed human victim being given to it. The Inca mummies were brought out for processions and other very solemn rites and ceremonies. When the Spanish destroyers came, the unfortunate people concealed the mummies of their beloved sovereigns, but the ferret-eyed Polo de Ondegardo searched diligently, and succeeded in accounting for all but one. The body of the great warrior statesman, Yupanqui Pachacuti, was finally buried in the court of the hospital of San Andres at Lima. Yahuar Huaccac, the stolen child, alone escaped desecration. His body was never found.

The Orejones and other important people were generally interred in caves, Machay, with two chambers, one for the mummy with his 'brother' or *Lar*, the other for his property, and for the offerings brought by the people. These caves were in desert places or on the sides of mountains. The heights overlooking the lovely valley of Yucay, called TTANTANA MARCA, are literally honeycombed with these burial caves. All have been desecrated by the Spaniards in search for treasure.

This curious belief in a spiritual essence of all the things that concerned the daily well-being of the people explains the multiplicity of *huacas*, or objects of worship. Every household had a *Sara Mama* to represent the spiritual essence of the maize, to which prayers and sacrifices were made. Sometimes it was a figure covered with cobs of maize, at others it was merely a vase fashioned as a cob. In like manner there was a *Llama Mama* for the flocks. More especially was the spirit of the earth itself, the *Pacha Mama*, an object of worship. The offerings consisted of the figures of llamas roughly fashioned. There was a cavity in their backs into which the sacrificial offering was placed, and they were buried in the fields. The offerings were chicha, spirits, or coca, the things the poor husbandman loved best. Dr. Max Uhle and the Princess Theresa of Bavaria have discovered that the ceremony of offering these things to *Pacha Mama* still prevails, in spite of the priests. The llamas of stone or clay are even offered for sale in the markets; Dr. Uhle saw them at Sicuani. The present practice is to bury the figures, with offerings, in the places where flocks of llamas or alpacas feed. The figure is placed between stones, and covered with another stone. Each year the offering is renewed by another figure, which is placed below the old one and nearer the *Pacha Mama,* This kind of sacrifice is called *Chuya.* It shows that the ancient beliefs and customs of the Peruvian Indians cannot be eradicated by any amount of persecution.

The religion of the ancient Peruvians was composed of several beliefs, all more or less peculiar to the Andean people, except the worship of a Supreme Being; which, however, only prevailed among the higher and more intellectual minds. Some of the Incas undoubtedly sought earnestly for a knowledge of the great First Cause, which they called Uira-cocha. The worship of the fabulous ancestor or originator of each *ayllu,* or clan, was universal, and as the sun was the accepted ancestor of the sovereign, its cult took the precedence of all others. The peculiar belief in the existence of a spiritual essence of all the things that concerned their well-being prevailed among the mass of the people, and has never been eradicated. It accounts for their innumerable *huacas* and household gods, and for the way in which the idea of the presence of the supernatural was inextricably mingled with all the actions of their lives. From these various beliefs and cults, firmly established in the minds and hearts of all classes of the people, we may gather some idea of the causes which led to the establishment among them of a government based on the system of *ayllus* or village communities. The rooted beliefs in the *Paccarisca* or common ancestry of each *ayllu,* placed their village system on a very firm basis, and as the Incas confirmed all local usages and superstitions of their subjects, a feeling of devoted loyalty appears to have been combined with veneration for the sun, the ancestor of their sovereigns. It is clear that the religious beliefs of the people were in perfect harmony with the remarkable social system on which the Inca government was based.

CHAPTER IX. THE INCA CALENDAR, FESTIVALS, AND DRESS OF THE SOVEREIGN AND HIS QUEEN

RELIGION, in its ritual and ceremonial observances, was dependent on the annual recurrence of agricultural events such as the preparation of the land, sowing, and harvest, and both were dependent on the calendar. In the records of the old kings the gradual improvements in calculating the coming and going of the seasons are recorded, and under the Incas a certain approach to accuracy had been attained. The solstices and equinoxes were carefully observed.

Stone pillars were erected, eight on the east and eight on the west side of Cuzco, to observe the solstices. They were in double rows, four and four, two low between two high ones, twenty feet apart. At the heads of the pillars there were discs for the sun's rays to enter. Marks were made on the ground, which had been levelled and paved. Lines were drawn to mark the movements of the sun, as shown when its rays entered the holes in the pillars. The pillars were called *Sucanca*, from *Suca*, a ridge or furrow, the alternate lights and shades appearing like furrows.

To ascertain the time of the equinoxes there was a stone column in the open space before the temple of the sun, in the centre of a large circle. A line was drawn across the paved area from east to west. The observers watched where the shadow of the column was on the line from sunrise to sunset, and when there was no shadow at noon. This instrument was called *Inti-huatana*, which means the place where the sun is tied up or encircled. There are also *Inti-huatanas* on the height of Ollantay-tampu, at Pissac, at Hatuncolla, and in other places.

The ancient name of the sun was *Uilca*. As a deity it was *Inti*. As the giver of daylight it was *Punchau*, or *Lupi*.

The name of the moon as a deity was *Pacsa Mama*; as giving light by night, *Quilla*; and there were names for its different phases.

Illapa was the name for thunder, lightning and thunderbolts, the servants of the sun. *Chuqui Yllayllapa, Chuqui Ilia Inti, Illapa* were names for the thunder god. *Liviac* was the lightning.

The stars were observed and many were named. Valera gives the names of five planets; and fifteen other names are given by Acosta, Balboa, Morua, and Calancha. An attempt to make out the twelve signs of the zodiac from these names of stars is unsupported by evidence that can be accepted. The only observations of celestial bodies for which there is conclusive testimony are those of the sun, for fixing the time of solstices and equinoxes.

The year was called *Huata*, the word *Huatana* being a halter, from *Huatani*, I seize; 'the place where the sun is tied up or encircled,' hence *Huata* means a year. The Peruvian year was divided into twelve *Quilla*, or moons, of thirty days. Five days were added at the end, called *Allcacanquis*. The rule for adding a day every fourth year kept the calendar correct. The monthly moon revolutions were finished in 354 days, 8 hours, 48 minutes. This was made to correspond with the solar year by adding eleven days, which were divided among the months. They regulated the intercalation by marks placed on the horizon, to denote where the sun rose and set on the days of the solstices and equinoxes. Observations of the sun were taken each month.

There is some want of agreement among the authorities who give the names of the months. Some have the same names, but they are not given to the same months, while others have different names. After a careful analysis I have come to the conclusion that the list given by Calancha, Polo de Ondegardo, Acosta, Morua and Cobos, which is the one accepted by the second Council of Lima, is the most correct. Each one of the other authorities has more names in agreement with the Calancha list than with any other. Acosta is in complete agreement as far as he goes, but only gives eight months.

The correct calendar was, I believe, as follows:

June 22 to July 22. INTIP RAYMI (*June* 22), Winter Solstice. *Harvest Festival.*
July 22 to Aug. 22. CHAHUAR QUIS.

Aug. 22 to Sept. 22. CCAPAC SITUA (*Sept.* 22), Spring Equinox. *Expiatory Festival.*
Sept. 22 to Oct. 22. CCOYA KAYMI (*Sept.* 22), Spring Equinox.
Oct. 22 to Nov. 22. UMA RAYMI.
Nov. 22 to Dec. 22. AYAMARCA (*Dec.* 22), Summer Solstice. Or CANTARAY.
Dec. 22 to Jan. 22. CCAPAC RAYMI (*Dec.* 22), Summer Solstice. *Huarachicu Festival.*
Jan. 22 to Feb. 22. CAMAY.
Feb. 22 to March 22. HATUN PUCUY (*March* 22), Autumn Equinox. *Great ripening.*
March 22 to April 22. PACHA PUCUY (*March* 22), Autumn Equinox. *Mosoc Nina.*
April 22 to May 22. AYRIHUA.
May 22 to June 22. AYMURAY (*June* 22), Winter Solstice. *Harvest.*

Gold plates $5^3/_{10}$ inches in diameter, representing the sun, with a border apparently designed to denote the months by special signs, were worn on the breast by the Incas and the great councillors. The gold ornaments were seized and ruthlessly destroyed by the Spaniards wherever they could be found. A great number were never found. Some were presented to General Echenique, then President of Peru, in 1853. There was the golden breastplate, a gold *topu* or pin, the head with a flat surface about 4 in. by 2 in., covered with incised ornaments; four half-discs forming two globes and a long stalk, also a flat piece of gold with a long stalk. We thought that the flat piece like a leaf and the discs were from the golden garden of the sun, and a golden belt or fillet for the head. The President brought them to the house of Don Manuel Cotes, at Lima, for me to see, on October 25, 1853, and I made a copy of the golden breastplate and of the *topu*. The Señora Grimanesa Cotes (*née* Althaus), the most beautiful lady in Lima at that time, held the tracing paper while I made the copy. It was very thin, and the figures were stamped, being convex on the outer side and concave on the inner. The outer diameter was $5^3/_{10}$ inches, the inner 4 inches. This is by far the most interesting relic of the Incas that is known to us. I believe that the figures round the border represent the months, and that the five spaces separating them, one above and four below, are intended for the five intercalary days, *Allcacanquis*. In giving an account of the months and their festivals, I will place each figure taken from the border of the breastplate against the month which I would suggest that it represents, with a description.

INTIP RAYMI, the first month of the Peruvian year, begins at the winter solstice, on June 22. The sign of the gold breastplate occurs four times, for four months, two beginning and two ending with a solstice. The diamonds on the right and below perhaps indicate direction.

The great harvest festival of *Intip Raymi* is picturesquely described by Valera. The harvest had been got in. There was a great banquet in the *Cusi Pata*, one of the principal squares of Cuzco, when the Orejones renewed their homage.

Rising above the buildings to the north could be seen the beautiful façade of the palace of Pachacuti, with the sacred farm of Sausiru, and above them the precipice of the Sacsahuaman, crowned by the fortress. On the sides of the square were the temples to Uira-cocha, and other edifices built of stone and roofed with thatch. The images of Uira-cocha, of the Sun and of Thunder, were brought out and placed on their golden altars. Presently the Inca and the Ccoya entered the square at the head of a long procession, with the standard, the *Tupac Yauri*, or golden sceptre, and the royal weapons borne before them.

This central figure of the Sovereign Inca was constantly seen on all great occasions. With the help of the portraits at Santa Ana, of the sketches in the curious manuscript of Huaman Poma, and of descriptions, we can imagine the appearance of the Peruvian emperor.

Many generations of culture and of rule had produced men of a very different type from any Peruvian Indian of to-day. We see the Incas in the pictures at the church of Santa Ana at Cuzco. The colour of the skin was many shades lighter than that of the down-trodden descendants of their subjects; the forehead high, the nose slightly aquiline, the chin and mouth firm, the whole face majestic, refined, and intellectual. The hair was carefully arranged, and round the head was the sign of sovereignty. The *llautu* appears to have been a short piece of red fringe on the forehead, fastened round the head by two bands. It was habitually worn, but when praying the Inca took it off, and put it on the ground beside him. The ceremonial head-dress was the *mascapaycha*, a golden semicircular mitre on the front of which the *llautu* was fastened. Bright-coloured feathers were fixed on the sides, and a plume rose over the summit. Long golden ear-drops came down to the shoulders. The tunic and mantle varied in colour, and were made of the finest vicuña wool. In war the mantle was twisted and tied up, either over the left shoulder or round the waist. On the breast the Incas wore a circular golden breastplate representing the sun, with a border of signs for the months. The later Incas wore a very rich kind of brocade, in bands sewn together, forming a wide belt. The bands were in squares, each with an ornament, and as these ornaments were invariable there was probably some meaning attached to them.

The material was called *tocapu*, and was generally worn as a wide belt of three bands. Some of the Incas had the whole tunic of *tocapu*. The breeches were black, and in loose pleats at the knees. The *usutas*, or sandals, were of white wool.

The Inca, equipped for war, had a large square shield of wood or leather, ornamented with patterns, and a cloth hanging from it, also with a pattern and fringe. There was a loop of leather on the back, to pass the arm through. In one hand was a wooden staff about two feet long, with a bronze star of six or eight points fixed at one end—a most formidable war-club. In the other hand was a long staff with the battle-axe fixed at one end, called *huaman champi* or *cunca cuchun*. In public worship or festivals the imperial weapons were usually laid aside, and borne before the sovereign.

The *Ccoya*, or queen, wore the *lliclla*, or mantle, fastened across the chest by a very large golden *topu*, or pin, with head richly carved with ornaments and figures. The *lliclla*, or mantle, and *acsu*, or skirt, varied as regards colour. The head was adorned with golden circlets and flowers.

These magnificent dresses gave an air of imperial grandeur to the great festivals, while the attire of the other Incas and of the Orejones was only slightly less imposing.

The High Priest, being an ascetic, was never present, but the other priests, the augurs and diviners, were in attendance. The councillors, great lords and warriors, were all assembled, seated according to their order and precedence, the Inca being on a raised platform under a canopy. Presently there appeared an immense crowd of people who had come from all directions to take part in the festival. As soon as the homage and the sacrifices were finished the tables were placed, covered with white cotton cloths, and adorned with flowers.

The ACLLAS, or virgins of the sun, then appeared, dressed in white robes, with diadems of gold. They came to serve at the feast. Commencing with the Inca and the Ccoya, they gave to all abundantly, adding plenty of chicha. Finally they gave to each guest a piece of the *Illay Tanta*, or sacred bread, which was looked upon as a precious gift, and preserved by the recipient as a relic.

After the feast the virgins brought the cloth they had been weaving during the whole year, and presented the best and most curious pieces to the Inca and the members of his family, then to the principal lords and their families. The cloth was all of vicuña wool, like silk. The virgins also presented robes, garlands, ornaments, and many other things. To the rest of the great assembly they distributed coarser cloth of wool and cotton. The harvest festivities were continued for several days.

Chahuar Quiz, the next month, from July 22 to August 22, was the season for ploughing the lands, without cessation and by relays. The sign on the breastplate seems to indicate that the work was continuous, both by the light of the sun, and of the moon and stars.

Ccapac Situa was the third month, the season for sowing the land. The sign on the breastplate indicates furrows on one side, and the act of pouring seed on a prepared plot of ground on the other. Another name for this month is *Yapaquis*, the word *Yapa* meaning an addition to land, or ploughed land, *Yapuna* being a plough. It was from August 22 to September 22.

Ccoya Raymi, from September 22 to October 22, was the fourth month, commencing with the vernal equinox. It was the month for the great nocturnal expiatory festival called SITUA. On the breastplate the signs represent the nocturnal character of the feast. The object of the festival was to pray to the Creator to be pleased to shield the people from sickness, and to drive all evils from the land.

A great number of men with lances, and fully armed for war, assembled in the *Intip Pampa*, or open space in front of the temple of the sun, where the High Priest proclaimed the feast. The armed men then shouted: 'O sickness, disaster and misfortune, go forth from the land!' Four hundred men assembled. They all belonged to *ayllus*, or clans, of the highest rank. Three *ayllus* of royal descent were represented, and four of those descending from the chosen followers of the *Ayars*. There were twenty to twenty-five selected from nineteen *ayllus*. One hundred faced to the south, one hundred to the west, one hundred to the east, and one hundred to the north. Again they shouted, 'Go forth, all evils!' Then all four companies ran with great speed in the directions they were facing. Those facing south ran as far as Acoyapuncu, about two leagues; finally bathing in the river at Quiquisana. Those facing west ran as far as the river Apurimac, and bathed there. Those facing east ran at full speed over the plateau of Chita and down into the Vilcamayu valley, bathing at Pissac. Those facing north ran in that direction 'until they came to a stream, where they bathed. The rivers were supposed to carry the evils to the sea.

When the ceremony commenced and the armed men started on their races, all the people came to their doors and, shaking their mantles, shouted: 'Let the evils be gone. Creator of all things, permit us to reach another year, that we may see another feast like this.' Including even the Inca, they all danced through the night, and went in the morning twilight to bathe in the rivers and fountains. They held great torches of straw bound round with cords, which they lighted and went on playing with them, passing them from one to the other. They were called *Pancurcu*. Meanwhile, puddings of coarsely ground maize, called *Sancu*, were prepared in every house. These puddings were applied to their faces and to the lintels of the doors, and were offered to the deities and to the mummies. On that day all, high and low, were to enjoy themselves, no man scolded his neighbour, and no word was passed in anger. On the following days there were magnificent religious ceremonials and sacrifices. Such was the great *Situa* festival.

Uma Raymi was the fifth month, from October 22 to November 22. It was so called because in this month the people of Uma, two leagues from Cuzco, celebrated their feast of *Huarachicu*. This was the month of brewing chicha, referring to a method of brewing chicha used at great festivals. The figure on the breastplate seems to refer to the opening of hives and buds which took place in this month. But it was essentially the brewing month, and it must be confessed that the effects of the brewing were a very prominent feature at all the festivals.

A fermented liquor was made from maize, which is called chicha by the Spaniards, but the native name is *acca*. The grains of maize were first chewed into a pulp by women and girls, because it was believed that saliva had medicinal qualities. The masticated maize was then boiled and passed through several colanders of fine cotton, and the liquor was finally expressed. Fermentation then took place. The *acca* was often flavoured with the berries of the *Schinus Molle* and other things to give it piquancy. Latterly the Peruvians discovered some kind of distilling process, and made a spirit called *uinapu* or *sora*. Drinking to excess prevailed at all the festivals, while the man who drank much and kept his head was held in high esteem. This prevalence of drunkenness at the festivals led to other vices, and was the most pernicious habit they indulged in.

Ayamarca, the sixth month, from November 22 to December 22, ended with the summer solstice, and had a sign on the breastplate similar to the month of the winter solstice. The name is that of a once powerful tribe near Cuzco, which held their *Huarachicu* festival in this month. In Cuzco it was a time of preparation for the great *Huarachicu* festival in the following month. Quantities of chicha continued to be brewed after the *Cantaray* fashion, whatever that may have been. The youths who were to receive their arms in the next month, went to the very sacred *huaca* called HUANACAURI to offer sacrifices and ask his permission to receive knighthood. This *huaca* was on a hill about three miles from Cuzco, and was one of the *Ayars*, brother of Manco Ccapac, turned into stone. It specially presided over the *Huarachicu* festival. The youths passed the night on the sacred hill, and fasted.

Ccapac Raymi, from December 22 to January 22, was the seventh month, beginning with the summer solstice. On the breastplate it has the solstitial sign, with the diamonds pointing differently. In this month was the grandest *Raymi*, or festival, in the year, called *Huarachicu*.

After going through an ordeal, the youths were given arms, allowed to wear breeches, called *huara*, and had their ears pierced. During the first eight days of the month all the relations were busily employed in preparing the *usutas*, or shoes made of fine reeds almost of the colour of gold, and the *huaras* of the sinews of llamas, and in embroidering the shirts in which the youths were to appear when they went to the hill of *Huanacauri*. The shirts were made of fine yellow wool with black borders of still finer wool like silk. The youths also wore mantles of white wool, long and narrow, reaching to the knees. They were fastened round the neck by a cord from whence hung a red tassel. The youths were clothed in this dress, shorn, and taken to the great square by their parents and relations. The latter wore yellow mantles with black plumes on their heads from a bird called *guito*. Many young maidens also came, aged from eleven to fourteen, of the best families, carrying vases of chicha. They were called *Ñusta-calli-sapa*, or princesses of unequalled valour. The images of the deities were brought out, and the youths and maidens, with their relations, were grouped around.

The Inca came forth, and the youths obtained permission from him to sacrifice to *Huanacauri*. Each had a llama prepared as an offering, and they all marched, with their relations, to the sacred hill. That night they slept at a place called Matahua, at the foot of the hill. At dawn next day they delivered up their offerings to the TARPUNTAY and ascended the hill, still fasting. This was the prayer they offered to the *Huanacauri*:

'O HUANACAURI, our Father, may the Creator, the Sun, and the Thunder ever remain young, and never become old. May thy son, the Inca, ever retain his youth, and grant that he may prosper in all his undertakings. To us, thy sons, who now celebrate this festival, grant that we may be ever in the hands of the Creator and in thy hands.'

Bags called *chuspas* were then given to the youths, and breeches made of aloe fibre and sinews of llamas, called *huara*. The youths then marched to a ravine called *Quirirmanta*, where they were met by their relations and severely flogged to try their endurance. This was followed by the song called *Huari*, the youths standing and the rest of the people seated. They returned to Cuzco, where the youths were flogged again in the great square. Then there was a curious ceremony. The shepherd of the llamas dedicated to the feast came with a llama, called *Napa*, draped in red cloth with golden earrings. It was preceded by men blowing through sea-shells. The *Suntur Paucar*, insignia of the Inca, was brought out, and a dance was performed. The youths and their relations then returned to their homes and fed upon the roasted flesh of the sacrificial llamas.

The business of initiation continued through the month. The next event was the great foot-race. The youths passed the night in a gorge called Quilli-yacolvaca, the starting-place being a hill, two leagues from Cuzco, called Anahuarqui. Each held a staff called *Tupac Yauri*, mounted with gold or bronze. Here five lambs were sacrificed to the Creator and the sun, followed by songs. The course was a very long one, as far as Huanacauri, where the maidens were stationed, called *Ñusta-calli-sapa*, with supplies of chicha to refresh the exhausted runners. They kept singing a refrain: 'Come quickly, youths, we are waiting for you.' The youths stood in a row at the foot of the hill, numbering several hundreds. The starter was an official gorgeously attired, and as he dropped the *Yauri* about eight hundred aspirants ran like deer across the plain—a thrilling sight. Few people, in the new or old world, could equal the Peruvians in speed, and the competition to be the first to receive drinks from the hands of beauty was very close. There were more songs and disciplinary flogging, and in the evening the grand procession was formed to return to Cuzco, headed by the *Suntur Paucar* of the Inca and the *Raymi Napa*, or golden llama.

On the next day the rewards were distributed by the Inca in person, on the hill called *Raurana*. The aspirants had passed the night in a place called *Huaman Cancha* (place of falcons), at the foot of the hill, which is two miles from Cuzco. The Inca proceeded to the summit of the hill, where stood the *huaca* called *Raurana*, consisting of two falcons carved in stone, upon an altar. The priest of the *huaca* officiated at the preliminary prayers and sacrifices, the youths standing in rows before their sovereign. There were prayers that the aspirants might become valiant and enterprising warriors. The *haylli* was sung and, at a sign from the Inca, the priest presented each of the youths with breeches called *huarayuru*, ear-pieces of gold, red mantles with blue tassels, and red shirts. They also received diadems with plumes called *pilco cassa*, and pieces of gold and silver to hang round their necks. Then followed songs and hymns, which lasted for an hour. The return to Cuzco was in the same order as on the previous day.

Next there was a grand performance in the *Huacay Pata*, or principal square of Cuzco. The skins of jaguars and pumas had been prepared with the heads, having gold pieces in their ears, golden teeth, and golden rings, called *chipana*, on their paws. Those who were dressed in the skins, with many other men and women, performed a ceremonial dance to the music of drums. The dance was performed with a cable, which was kept in a building called *Moro Urco*, near the temple of the sun. The cable was woven in four colours—black, white, red, and yellow. At the ends there were stout balls of red wool. All over the strands small plates of gold and silver were sewn. The cable was called *Huascar*. Every one took hold of it, men on one side disguised in the skins and heads of wild beasts, and women on the other, and so, to the sounds of wild music, the *Yaqauyra* was danced through a great part of the night, round and round until the dancers were in the shape of a spiral shell, and then unwinding. Finally the cable was taken back to the *Moro Urco*.

Next, in the third week of the month, all the youths went to bathe in the fountain called *Calis Puquio*, about a mile to the rear of the fortress of Cuzco, in the ravine of the Huatanay. They returned to the *Huacay Pata*, and were solemnly presented with their arms, the sling, the club, the axe, and the shield, the ceremony concluding with prayers and sacrifices. The final event was the boring of the ears, which completed the transition from boys to fully equipped Orejones and warriors. Next came the use of the weapons.

The next month, from January 22 to February 22, was called *Camay*. It was the month of exercises and sham fights. The youths were divided into two armies of Hanan Cuzco and Hurin Cuzco, and on the very first day they came into the great square with the *Huaracas*, or slings, and began to hurl stones at each other. At times they came to close quarters to try the strength of their muscles. The Inca was himself present in person, and preserved order; seeing also that the young warriors were taught to march together, and to use the axe and the club. During these exercises the new knights wore black tunics, fawn-coloured mantles, and a head-dress of white feathers from a bird called *tocto*. After the exercises there was a feast, with much drinking of chicha.

The ninth month was the month of the great ripening. It was called *Hatun Pucuy*, and was represented by stalks of corn with curved baskets. Betanzos has *Colla Pucuy*. Both names refer to the ripening.

Pacha Pucuy was the tenth month, from March 22 to April 22, at the autumnal equinox. In this month there was the fourth great annual festival called the *Mosoc Nina*, when the sacred fire in the temple, always kept burning, was solemnly renewed. The month is represented by the stone and the spark.

The *Ayrihua*, from April 22 to May 22, was the beginning of harvest. The new knights went to the foot of the fortress, to the farm called SAUSIRU. The tradition was that here the wife of the Ayar Manco

Ccapac sowed the first maize. They returned with the maize in small baskets, singing the *Yarahui*.

The twelfth and last month of the year was called *Aymuray*, and was the month for gathering in the harvests and conveying the corn and other produce to the barns and store-houses. Huaman Poma gives a picture of the busy scene. The month is represented by the solstitial sign, because its last day is the solstice. Then followed the great harvest-home month of *Intip Raymi*.

Besides the great festivals which came round with the calendar, the Peruvians had their family rites and ceremonies. On the fourth day after the birth of a child, all the relations were invited to come and see it, in its *Quirau* or cradle. When it reached the age of one year, it was given a name, whether boy or girl, to last until it was of age. This was called the *Rutuchicu*. The child was then shorn, the eldest uncle cutting the first hair. At the *Huarachicu* the youth dropped his child name, and received another name to last for his life. Girls, when they were of age, had to undergo a ceremony called *Quicuchica*. They had to fast for three days, and on the fourth they were washed and clothed in a dress called *Ancalluasu*, with shoes of white wool. Their hair was plaited and a sort of bag was placed on their heads. The relations then came, and gave the girl the name she was to bear for the rest of her life. They presented gifts, but there were no idolatrous practices.

In all this we see how the family rites, and the festivals coming round with the months, were woven into the lives of the people; and, at least at Cuzco, the central figure of the sovereign Inca rose above it all, constantly seen as the chief person in all that concerned them.

During the palmy days of the empire the festivals were observed in each province, though, of course, with less magnificence, under the auspices of the Viceroys and Curacas.

CHAPTER X. LANGUAGE AND LITERATURE OF THE INCAS

IT was the wise policy of the Incas to try to establish one language throughout their vast dominions, and they had an excellent instrument for their purpose. Their language was called *Runa-simi*, literally, the 'man's mouth,' or, as we should say, the man's tongue or the human speech. It was spoken, in its perfection, in the Inca and Quichua regions, the lands watered by the Vilcamayu and the Apurimac, with their tributaries. But the speech of more distant tribes was closely allied, and merely formed dialects, so that the establishment of the use of the *Runa-simi* presented but slight difficulties. Indeed, I am inclined to think that the separate dialects were the debris of one original language spoken during the megalithic age. Differences would be caused by the isolation of *ayllus* in valleys difficult of access. The same words would receive different meanings, while different words would get to have the same meaning.

It was the object of the rulers of Peru that these differences should disappear, and this useful administrative measure was quickly and automatically nearing completion. The *Runa-simi* is a rich and flexible language. It would be tedious to enter into much detail, but a few peculiarities may be mentioned. The letters B, D, F, and G (hard) are wanting, and the vowels E and are rarely used. But there are some forcible gutturals, and some words require a very strong emphasis on the initial P and T. The sound Ch is frequent. In the grammar there are no genders, no articles, and the particle, which forms the plural of nouns, is declined. The verbs have two first persons plural, inclusive and exclusive, and particles which have the effect of indicating transition from the first person to the second, second to third, third to first, and third to second. But the peculiarity in the language which gives it such great power of expression and flexibility is the use of nominal and verbal particles. They are exceedingly numerous, serving to alter the parts of speech, and to modify the meanings of words in an infinite number of ways. As is the case with some other American languages, there is a great variety of names for degrees of relationship. For instance, there is a different word for the sister of a brother and the sister of a sister, and *vice versâ*.

The *Runa-simi* was well adapted for administrative purposes, such as promulgating decrees, recording statistics, and keeping accounts. For the latter purposes the Peruvians resorted to the use of *quipus*. I am unable to throw any new light on the extent to which this system could be made to record events, except that further evidence has been forthcoming that they were actually used for such purposes. For administrative work their utility cannot be doubted, and they served their purpose admirably. The *quipu* was a rope to which a number of strings were attached, on which knots were made to denote numbers units, tens, hundreds, &c. The Peruvians had a complete system of numeration. The colours of the strings explained the subjects to which the numbers referred. The accounts were in charge of trained officials called *Quipucamayoc*, and by this method the complicated business of a great empire was conducted.

It is quite conceivable that, with a sufficient staff of trained and competent officials, such a system might be made to work efficiently. Indeed, we know that this was the case. The difficulty is to understand how traditions could be preserved and historical events recorded by the use of *quipus*. Blas Valera refers, as his authorities for various statements respecting rites and ceremonies, to the *quipus* preserved in different provinces, and even by private persons.

There must, however, have been interpreters of the *quipus*, those who, with knowledge derived from other sources, could use the knots as reminders and suggesters by which an event could be kept in memory with more accuracy. These were the *Amautas*, or learned men and councillors. For them the *quipus* formed a system of reminders, giving accuracy to knowledge derived from other methods of recording events and traditions. For it cannot be supposed that the system of different coloured knots could do more than supply a sort of aid to memory, or a *memoria technica*. It is, however, certain that the traditions and records of events were preserved by the *Amautas* with considerable exactness. There is, for instance, the Paccari-tampu myth. It is told by Garcilasso de la Vega, Cieza de Leon, Betanzos, Balboa, Morua, Montesinos, Salcamayhua and Sarmiento, all agreeing sufficiently closely to prove that precisely the same tradition had been handed down, with the same details, to their various informants. Similarly the details of the Chanca war and other principal events were preserved.

Sarmiento tells us how this was done on the highest authority. He examined thirty-two witnesses of the Inca family in 1571, and his first inquiry was respecting the way in which the memory of historical events was preserved. He was informed that the descendants of each sovereign formed an *ayllu* or family, whose duty it was to keep the records of the events of his reign. This was done by handing down the histories in the form of narratives and songs which the *Amautas* of each *ayllu*, specially trained for the duty, learnt by heart from generation to generation. They had help by means of the *quipus*, and also by the use of pictures painted on boards. These pictures, it was stated, were preserved with great care. But none have come down to us. Pictures are mentioned by Garcilasso de la Vega, and there are entries in the recently discovered manuscript of Huaman Poma which make it almost certain that portraits of the Incas and their queens once existed. Huaman Poma gives clever pen-and-ink sketches of the Incas and Ccoyas, with a page of description for each. In the descriptions he not only gives an account of the personal appearance, but also mentions the colour of the tunic and mantle of each Inca, and of the *acsu* and *lliclla* of each Ccoya. Now this would be quite out of place for pen-and-ink sketches. It is, therefore, fairly certain that Huaman Poma alluded to coloured pictures, or to the tradition of them, and that such pictures were used to assist and confirm the traditions handed down in the *ayllus*, with the aid of the *quipus*. The preservation of the traditions and lists of the ancient kings, as well as of the historical events in the reigns of the Incas, were secured by these means. Sarmiento tells us that the most notable historical events were painted on great boards and deposited in the hall of the temple of the sun. Learned persons were appointed, who were well versed in the art of understanding and explaining them.

The Peruvians appear to have been advanced in the study of geography and in the use of relief maps. The provinces were measured and surveyed, and the natural features were shown by means of these relief maps moulded in clay. They were used by the Incas for administrative purposes, and especially for deciding the destinations of colonists. Garcilasso de la Vega had the great advantage of seeing one of these relief maps. It was made of clay, with small stones and sticks, and was a model of the city of Cuzco, showing the four main roads. It was according to scale, and showed the squares and streets, and the streams, and the surrounding country with its hills and valleys. The Inca declares that it was well worthy of admiration, and that the best cosmographer in the world could not have done it better. It was constructed at Muyna, a few leagues south of Cuzco, where Garcilasso saw it.

There were *Yacha Huasi*, or schools, at Cuzco, said to have been founded by Inca Rocca, where youths were trained and instructed as *Amautas* and *Quipucamayocs*. The former were in close touch with the hierarchy, and were usually either priests or councillors of the sovereign. The *Harahuecs*, or bards, were also trained at these institutions.

The *Runa-simi* was nobly and abundantly used in preserving the origins and developments of Andean civilisation, although the want of knowledge of an alphabet and the Spanish cataclysm have only allowed that preservation, so complete when the end came, to reach us in scattered fragments. Probably the most ancient relic we possess is the mythical song given by Valera, and handed down to us by Garcilasso de la Vega. It is a fanciful idea, referring the noise of thunder to the shattering of a sister's bowl by a brother; a slight thing in itself, but showing the play of fancy in the imaginative minds of these people. Of equal antiquity are the prayers which have been preserved by Molina, and those hymns to the Supreme Being handed down to us by Salcamayhua. A pretty harvest song, a hunting song to accompany a dance, a love ditty, and a remarkable song supposed to be sung by a condemned man before execution, are undoubtedly ancient, for they are found in the manuscript of Huaman Poma. They throw much light on the simple character of the people, on their fancies and turns of thought. The love song is imaginative, and has some pretty fancies. There were many such songs in the collection of Dr. Justiniani, and some occur in the drama of Ollantay.

The most interesting and complete relic of Peruvian literature is the drama of Ollantay, over which there has been much controversy with reference to its antiquity. It was first made known through the account of it given in the 'Museo Erudito' of Cuzco, in 1837. In 1853 the present writer made search for the original text of the drama, and for the best sources of information. In those days an intelligent and learned scholar, Dr. Julian Ochoa, was Rector of the University of San Antonio Abad at Cuzco, and there also resided in the ancient city of the Incas a venerable lady who remembered the insurrection of Pumacagua, and whose intimate relations with the leading Indians of those times, and profound knowledge of the folklore and language of her countrymen, placed her in the first rank as an exponent of tradition. It was under the guidance of these two high authorities that the present writer conducted his researches.

They told him of the existence of a last descendant of the Incas, living in one of the most secluded valleys of the eastern Andes, and possessing the original text of the old Inca drama, and many other documents of interest. It was necessary to cross the lofty range of mountains which bounds the lovely vale of the Vilcamayu, to pass over grassy plateaux at a great elevation, where the sapphire blue of the small alpine lakes contrasted with the dark surfaces of the precipitous cliffs, and then to descend, by winding paths, into the secluded vale of Laris. Here there was a small church, a few huts, and a house consisting of buildings on two sides of a courtyard, with the church tower seen over the roof. Away in one direction there was a wooded glen of great depth, containing one small house built over a spring, which consists of medicinal waters of special virtue for various complaints. A small stream flowed down another ravine of wonderful beauty, with lofty mountains on either side. In those days the downward course of the river, called the Yanatilde, was unknown. Recently it has been explored, and found to be a tributary of the Vilcamayu.

Such was Laris, where the descendant of the Incas lived as cura of the parish, with his grandniece. His name was Dr. Pablo Justiniani, in direct descent from the Princess Maria Usca, married to Pedro Ortiz de Orue, the Encomendero of Maras. It will perhaps be remembered that Maras was the name of one of the tribes which followed the Ayars from Paccari-tampu. Dr. Justiniani was a very old man. He could remember the great rebellion of Tupac Amaru in 1782, and was a friend of Dr. Antonio Valdez, who reduced the drama of Ollantay to writing.

His house consisted of a long room opening on the courtyard, with small rooms at each end, and a kitchen in the other building. The furniture was a long table, some very old chairs, an inlaid cabinet, and two ancient chests. Round the walls hung portraits of all the Incas from Manco Ccapac to Tupac Amaru, including the Princess Maria Usca. Under the portrait of Tupac Amaru was the sentence in Quichua: 'O Lord! behold how my enemies shed my blood.' There were also the coats of arms of the Incas granted by the Emperor Charles V, of Ortiz de Orue, Gonzalez, Carbajal, and Justiniani.

The old cura talked of the drama of Ollantay, of Inca literature, and of the rebellions of Tupac Amaru and Pumacagua. His guest, in the intervals of copying manuscripts, took long rambles down the beautiful vale of Yanatilde, and rejoiced to see the friendly relations that existed between the old cura and his parishioners, who raised crops of potatoes and ocas, and kept flocks of llamas which found pasturage on the mountain slopes. Bright and full of conversation in the daytime, the old cura sometimes suffered from headaches in the evenings. His niece then stuck coca leaves all over his forehead, which drove away the pain, so that he literally enjoyed a green old age. This was before the discovery of the virtues of cocaine.

Out of the old cabinet, inlaid with mother-ofpearl and haliotis, Dr. Justiniani brought the pedigree showing his descent from the Incas, another pedigree showing his descent from the Emperor Justinian through the Genoese family, a volume of old Quichua songs, and the text of the drama of Ollantay. All these precious documents were diligently copied. He gave me an account of the reduction of the drama to writing, and of the existing copies.

It will be well to quote what Garcilasso de la Vega and others say on the subject before giving the information received from Dr. Justiniani: 'The Amautas composed both tragedies and comedies, which were represented before the Inca and his court on solemn occasions. The subject matter of the tragedy related to military deeds and the victories of former times; while the arguments of the comedies were on agricultural and familiar household subjects. They understood the composition of long and short verses, with the right number of syllables in each. They did not use rhymes in the verses.' Salcamayhua also bears witness to the existence of the ancient drama, and gives the names for four different kinds of plays called *Anay Sauca*, a joyous representation, *Hayachuca*, *Llama-llama*, a farce, and *Hanamsi*, a tragedy. There is a clear proof that the memory of the old dramatic lore was preserved, and that the dramas were handed down by memory after the Spanish conquest. It is to be found in the sentence pronounced on the rebels at Cuzco, by the Judge Areche, in 1781. It prohibited 'the representation of dramas, as well as all other festivals which the Indians celebrated in memory of their Incas.'

There then can be no doubt that these Inca dramas had been handed down. Dr. Justinian! told me that the Ollantay play was put into writing by Dr. Don Antonio Valdez, the cura of Sicuani, from the mouths of Indians. He divided it into scenes, with a few stage directions, and it was acted before the unfortunate Tupac Amaru, a friend of Valdez, who headed an insurrection against the Spaniards in 1782. It would appear that Valdez was not the first to reduce the play to writing, for there is or was a version of 1735, and others dating from the previous century.

The father of Dr. Justiniani was a friend of Dr. Valdez, and he made a copy of that learned Quichua scholar's manuscript. This is the one which I copied. Dr. Valdez died in 1816, and in 1853 the original Valdez manuscript was possessed by his nephew and heir, Don Narciso Cuentas of Tinta. I ascertained the existence of another copy in the possession of Dr. Rosas, the cura of Chinchero, and there was another in the monastery of San Domingo at Cuzco, which was nearly illegible from damp. But the literature on the subject of the drama of Ollantay is extensive.

The period of the drama is during the reigns of the Inca Pachacuti and his son Tupac Yupanqui. The hero is a warrior named Apu Ollantay, who was Viceroy of the province of Anti-suyu. Though not of the blood-royal, this young nobleman entertained a sacrilegious love for a daughter of the Inca named Cusi Coyllur, or the 'joyful star.' The play opens with a dialogue between Ollantay and his servant Piqui Chaqui, a witty and facetious lad whose punning sallies form the comic vein which runs through the piece. Their talk is of Ollantay's love for the princess, and to them enters the High Priest of the Sun, who, by performing a miracle, endeavours to dissuade the audacious warrior from his forbidden love.

In the second scene the princess herself laments to her mother the absence of Ollantay. The Inca Pachacuti enters, and expresses warm affection for his child. Two songs are introduced, the first being a harvest song with a chorus threatening the birds that rob the corn, and the second a mournful love elegy.

The lover presses his suit upon the Inca in the third scene, and is scornfully repulsed. He bursts out into open defiance in a soliloquy of great force. Then there is an amusing dialogue with Piqui Chaqui, and another love song concludes the act. Ollantay collects an army of Antis, and occupies the impregnable fortress in the valley of the Vilcamayu, since called Ollantay-tampu, accompanied by two other chiefs named Urco Huaranca and Hanco Huayllu. Meanwhile Cusi Coyllur gave birth to a female child named Yma Sumac (*How beautiful*), a crime for which she was immured in a dungeon by her enraged father, the Inca Pachacuti. The child is brought up in the same building, without being aware of the existence of her mother.

Ollantay-tampu, at the entrance of a ravine descending to the valley of the Vilcamayu, rises amidst scenery of indescribable loveliness. The mountain of the principal ruins is very lofty and in the form of a sugar loaf, but with narrow plateaux breaking the steep slope, and giving room for the buildings. There is now little left, and their unusual arrangement, which was made a necessity by the peculiarity and narrowness of the sites, makes it difficult to comprehend the original plan. Moreover the ruins are of different periods, some certainly belonging to the megalithic age.

Ollantay-tampu was the fortress defending the sacred valley from the incursions of wild tribes from the north. It is the most interesting ruin in Peru, whether from an historical or a legendary point of view. It was the scene of this famous Inca drama, and here the gallant young Inca Manco repulsed the attack of the Spaniards under Hernando Pizarro.

A fairly wide ravine, called Marca-cocha, descends from the heights of the Andes to the Vilcamayu valley, and at its entrance two lofty mountains rise on either side, with the little town of Ollantay-tampu between them. A steep path leads up, for 300 feet, to the first small plateau covered with ruins. On this little level space there are five immense stone slabs, upright against the mountain side. They stand endways, twelve feet high, united by small smooth pieces fitted between them. At their bases there are other blocks of huge dimensions, one fifteen feet long. I believe this to have been the great hall of the fortified palace of Ollantay. A stone staircase leads down to a small plateau, which was another part of the interior.

Immediately below these plateaux there is a very remarkable terrace, with a wall of polygonal stones fitting exactly into each other, the lower course formed of blocks of immense size. In the wall there are nine recesses, 2 ft. 2 ins. high by 1 ft. 4 ins. by 1 ft. 1 in. deep, to hold the household gods. At the further end the terrace is approached by a handsome doorway with a monolithic lintel, the side of immense stones sloping slightly inwards. A long staircase, hewn out of the solid rock, leads down. This doorway and terrace were the chief entrance and vestibule of the palace. Below the terrace there is a succession of well-constructed *andeneria*, or cultivated terraces, sixteen deep, descending to the valley. They would have supplied the garrison with provisions.

Beyond the second plateau, which I believe to have been an interior, there is an open space which formed a court in front of the palace, and extended to the brink of a precipice which is partly revetted with masonry, whence there is a lovely view over the valleys. High up, above the palace, was the *Inti-huatana*, or circle and pillar for observing the equinox, like that which was formerly in the *Inti-pampa* at Cuzco.

About half a mile up the Marca-cocha ravine the cliff becomes perpendicular, and here giant seats have been excavated, having canopies and steps up to them, with connecting galleries, all hewn out of the solid rocks. One is called *Ñusta-tiana* (the princess's seat), the other *Inca-misana*, from its resemblance to an altar. On the road from the quarry there are two hewn stones called the *saycusca rumi-cuna* (tired stones). One is 9 ft. 8 ins. by 7 ft. 8 ins., the other 20 ft. by 15 ft. by 3 ft. 6 ins. The excavations, the tired stones, and parts of the ruins date from the megalithic age. The rest may be of the period of Ollantay.

The second act finds Ollantay in open rebellion, and fully established in this wonderful palace, where he was engaged in building and fortifying for several years. The name may be either from the drama or from an actual event handed down by tradition, but most of the early writers only call the fortress 'Tampu' without any prefix. Molina and Salcamayhua have the complete name, Ollantay-tampu. The second act opens with Ollantay in his stronghold, hailed as Inca by his followers.

In the next scene Yma Sumac, the child of Ollantay and Cusi Coyllur, who had been brought up without being aware of her mother's existence, is conversing with her attendant, Pitu Salla. The girl tells of the groans and sighs she has heard, when she has been walking in the garden, and of the strange feelings with which they fill her mind. Her speech is the finest passage in the play. There is an amusing dialogue between Rumi-ñaui, the general of Colla-suyu, and the scapegrace Piqui Chaqui, in the third scene, during which the death of the Inca Pachacuti is announced. He was succeeded by his son Tupac Yupanqui, who had been absent for many years, engaged in conquests, and is supposed to have been imperfectly informed of the events that had taken place round Cuzco. The new Inca gave the command of an army to Rumi-ñaui, with the duty of reducing the rebel forces under Ollantay to subjection.

In the last act Rumi-ñaui adopted a cunning stratagem. Concealing his army in the neighbouring ravine of Yana-huara, he came to the stronghold of the rebels, and appeared before Ollantay with his face covered with blood. He declared that he had been ill-treated by the Inca, and that he wished to join the insurrection. With regard to this incident, it is recorded that, in 1837, an Indian presented to Don Antonio Maria Alvarez, the political chief of Cuzco, an earthen vase with a face moulded on it. The portrait must have been that of a general, from the *mascapaycha*, or head-dress, and there were cuts on the face. The Indian declared that it had been handed down in his family, from generation to generation, as the likeness of the general Rumi-ñaui.

Rumi-ñaui was received as an old friend and companion by Ollantay. A few days afterwards the great festival of *Intip Raymi* was celebrated. Rumi-ñaui encouraged the drunken orgies, keeping sober himself, and when all were heavy with liquor he opened the gates to admit his own men, and made prisoners of Ollantay and all his followers.

In the next scene there is a touching dialogue between Yma Sumac and Pitu Salla, which ends in the child being allowed to visit her mother in the dungeon.

The successful stratagem of Rumi-ñaui is reported to the Inca, in the next scene, by a messenger. Ollantay and his companions are then brought in as prisoners by the victorious general, who recommends that they should be put to death. But the magnanimous Inca not only pardons them, but restores Ollantay to all his honours. In the midst of the ceremonies' of reconciliation, the child Yma Sumac bursts into the presence and entreats the Inca to save the life of his sister and her mother. All proceed to the dungeon of Cusi Coyllur, who is supposed to have been long since dead. The unfortunate princess is restored to the arms of her lover, and they receive the blessing of their sovereign.

The drama of Ollantay is not alone in allowing a romantic passion to transgress the usages of the Inca court. We have another instance in the loves of Quilacu and Curi Coyllur, which are told in a subsequent chapter, and another given by Morua, in the love of the Princess CHUQUI-LLANTU for the shepherd-boy ACOYA-NAPA. It is most fortunate that this ancient drama has been preserved through having been reduced to writing by an appreciative scholar. The Inca Indians had a remarkable aptitude for dramatic representation, of which the Spanish priests took advantage. They collected Inca dramatic traditions and songs and compiled religious plays from them, in imitation of the *Autos Sacramentales* then in vogue. Garcilasso de la Vega mentions these religious plays, and adds that the 'Indian lads repeated the dialogues with so much grace, feeling, and correct action, that they gave universal satisfaction and pleasure, and with so much plaintive softness in the songs, that the audience shed tears of joy at seeing their skill and ability.'

I have two of these plays in my possession, written in the Quichua language. One was arranged by Dr. Lunarejo, a native of Cuzco and a celebrated Quichua scholar of the eighteenth century; but the date is 1707, before his time. It is entitled 'El pobre mas rico,' and was acted by

Indians at Cuzco, where the scene is laid, in the days of the Incas. The *dramatis personae* are:

    Nina Quiru Inca   Cora Siclla Ñusta
    Yauri Titu Inca   Cora Umina Ñusta
    Amaru Inca   An Angel
    Quespillo (a droll)   Demons.

 The other Quichua drama, entitled 'USCA PAUCAR,' is more ancient, and was given to me by Dr. Julian Ochoa of Cuzco; but it is strictly an *Auto Sacramental*. The *dramatis personae* are:

    Usca Paucar   Cheque Apu (an old man)
    Quespillo (a droll)   Ccori-ttica
    Luzvel Yuncanina   An Angel.

 I also have copies of twenty songs from the collection of Dr. Justiniani, and several others received from Quichua scholars in Ayacucho, Cuzco, and Puno. Nearly all are love songs, a few bright and cheerful, but the majority are elegies breathing sorrow and despair.

 The Incas were able to preserve the pedigrees and events of the reigns of sovereigns for many generations, by the means that have been described. In their dramas and songs they had made great advances in the poetic art, not only using verses to give expression to the passions of love and despair, but also to preserve fanciful myths and legends. In astronomy their knowledge sufficed to fix the periods of the solar year. The *Amautas* also had an extensive knowledge of the use of medicinal herbs and roots, and their advances in surgery are attested by the discovery of skulls at Yucay and elsewhere on which the trepanning operation has been performed. They used infusions of several herbs as purgatives and stomachics, as well as the root of a convolvulus; other herbs were used for colds and pulmonary complaints, and salves were used, consisting of leaves and seeds of certain plants dried, pounded, and mixed with lard, some for wounds, others for rheumatism. For fearers they used several tonics, including a gentian. The chinchona plant was certainly used locally as a febrifuge, but not, I think, universally. In the Loxa province the bark was used, and known as *Quina-quina*. In the forests of Caravaya an infusion of the Chinchona flowers was given for ague, and called *Yara chucchu*. The name of *calisaya*, the species richest in quinine, is derived from two Quichua words: *Ccali*, strong, and *sayay*, to stand.

From time immemorial men of a tribe called Collahuaya or Charasani, from Upper Peru, have collected medicinal herbs and roots, and, as itinerant doctors, have carried them all over the empire of the Incas. I have collected all the names of medicinal herbs and roots from ancient authors, especially Cobos. I have also received information on the same subjects from people with whom I came in contact who were likely to know the herbs now used by the Indians; and I have examined the bags of the Collahuayas at Lampa and other places. It is an interesting fact that many of the remedies mentioned by ancient writers are still to be found in the bags of modern itinerant doctors. The Inca Garcilasso says that his mother's people used many medicinal plants, but he had forgotten their names. He, however, mentions the extraordinary effects of one called *matecllu*, which are described in the chapter on the Inca's life at page 268.

CHAPTER XI. CONDITION OF THE PEOPLE

THE history of the people who formed the empire of the Incas, in their earlier development, is well worthy of careful study. Sarmiento's version of what he was told by the *Amautas* was that the people were broken up into small tribes, living in what the Spaniards call *behetria*, without any government except in time of war, when a temporary chief, called *Sinchi*, was elected. But this is a very inadequate and misleading account of what must have been told him. The mountainous nature of the Andean region, cut up by such gorges as those of the Apurimac and the Pampas, led to the formation of numerous separate communities, and this would equally be the state of affairs in the valleys on the coast, which are separated from each other by sandy deserts.

These communities were not without government, as Sarmiento supposed. From remote antiquity they consisted of families, all being related, like the Roman *gens*. A single community, occupying part of a valley or a limited area, was called an *ayllu*. It was an organised family something on the lines of the village communities in India. The necessity for agricultural and pastoral industries led inevitably to a life of social intercourse, and to a patriarchal system under which, the land belonged to the *ayllu*. The arable land was assigned annually to the heads of families, while the pasture and woodland continued to be the common property of the *ayllu*. There were doubtless frequent wars respecting boundaries and rights of pasturage with neighbouring *ayllus*, but there were also confederations of *ayllus* for defence, and for the construction of works for the common good, which would be beyond the powers of a single *ayllu*—such as works of irrigation, and terraced cultivation. The unit was the head of a family, called *puric*, the united *purics* formed the *ayllu*, which occupied the cultivable land called *marca*.

There is abundant evidence that this patriarchal system, with rules established by long custom, had existed from remote antiquity. The development of agriculture and the domestication of animals could not have been continued for centuries without the existence of an ordered social life, pointing to a head or heads to rule and direct. Moreover, the traditions and ancestral descents of the *ayllus* were most carefully preserved down to the very last, and this no doubt led to the worship of ancestors, and to all the ceremonial services which it involved.

In course of time the neighbouring *ayllus*, in many instances, united not only for purposes of defence, but also for social and industrial objects, thus forming a *clan* composed of several *ayllus* or families. Then several clans united and became a powerful tribe with an hereditary chief. Finally there arose great confederations like those of the Incas, the Chancas, and the Collas; ending, after fierce and prolonged wars, in the supremacy of the Incas.

The Incas respected the organisations they found among the people who came under their rule, and did not disturb or alter the social institutions of the numerous tribes they conquered. Their statesmanship consisted in systematising the institutions which had existed from remote antiquity, and in adapting them to the requirements of a great empire.

Under the Incas the *ayllu* became a pachaca (100 families), over which was placed a *Llacta-camayoc* or village officer, whose duty it was to divide the *marca* annually into *topus*, three being assigned to each *puric* or head of a family, sufficient for the maintenance of himself and his people, and for the payment of tribute to the state and to religion; one third to each.

The *puric* was responsible for the maintenance of his family connections, who were divided into ten classes, with their women:

1. *Puñuc rucu* (old man sleeping), sixty years and upwards.
2. *Chaupi rucu* ('half old'), fifty to sixty years. Doing light work.
3. *Puric* (able-bodied), twenty-five to fifty. Tribute payer and head of the family.
4. *Yma huayna* (almost a youth), twenty to twenty-five. Worker.
5. *Coca palla* (coca picker), sixteen to twenty. Worker.
6. *Pucllac huamra*, eight to sixteen. Light work.

7. *Ttanta raquizic* (bread receiver), six to eight.
8. *Macta puric,* under six.
9. *Saya huamrac,* able to stand.
10. *Mosoc caparic,* baby in arms.

From all the classes younger than the *puric*, male and female, a certain number were taken annually for the service of the state and of religion. The population appears to have increased rapidly. In the *pachaca*, or old *ayllu*, there were a hundred *purics*. The *Llacta-camayoc* or head of the *pachaca* had to see that all were properly nourished and to register births and deaths.

Ten *pachacas* formed a *huaranca* (1000 families), with a chief selected from among the *llacta-camayocs*. The whole valley or district comprised a varying number of *huarancas* which was called a *hunu*, and the old hereditary native chiefs, with the name of *curacas*, retained some judicial power and were free from tribute. But over every four *hunus* there was an imperial officer called a *Tucuyricoc*, the literal meaning of which is 'He who sees all.' His duty as overseer was to see that the whole complicated system of administration worked with regularity, and that all the responsible officials under him performed their duties efficiently. The later Incas had a Viceroy of the blood-royal, called Ccapac Apu, for each of the four great provinces.

There was also a system of periodical visitors to overlook the census and the tribute, and to examine minutely and report upon the state of affairs in each district. Other visitors, in consultation with the local officials, selected young people of both sexes from the households of the *purics* for employments in the service of the State and of religion, according to their several aptitudes. Marriages were also arranged by the visiting officials.

From the ranks of the people, men and women were needed for many purposes of state, each chosen from out of a *puric* household. First there were the shepherds. A census was taken of all the llamas and alpacas in each district and they were divided into flocks for the state, for religion and sacrifices, and for the *curacas*. They were sent to the best pastures in charge of the shepherds, and each *puric* received two couples for breeding purposes. Other youths were required as hunters, soldiers, *chasquis* or messengers, road makers, builders, miners, artificers, and for the service of religion. Maidens were taken for the special service of the sun, selected by an official called *Apupanaca*. Servants, called *yana-cuna*, were latterly chosen in a different way. It appears that a small tribe, living on the banks of a stream called Yana-mayu (black river), had been guilty of some shocking treason to Tupac Inca, and was to be annihilated. But the queen interceded for them, and the sentence was commuted to servitude for themselves and their descendants. They were called *yana-mayu cuna*, which was soon corrupted into *yana-cuna*; and *yana* became the word for a domestic servant, as well as for the colour *black*. This institution of *yana-cuna* as domestic servants was quite exceptional, and no part of the regular Incarial system.

Not the least important part of that system was the policy of planting colonists, called *mitimaes*, especially in provinces recently conquered or supposed to be disaffected. Married young men from the *yma huayna* class, with their wives, were collected from a particular district and conveyed to a distant part of the empire, where their loyalty and industry would leaven a disaffected region. Vast numbers from recently conquered provinces were transported to localities where they would be surrounded by a loyal population, or to the eastern forests and unoccupied coast valleys. This was especially the case with the Collas, many of whom were sent as *mitimaes* or colonists as far as the borders of Quito. The Lupacas, on the western shores of Lake Titicaca, were exiled in great numbers to the southern coast valleys of Moquegua and Tacna. Their places were filled by loyal colonists from the Inca districts of Aymara, Cotapampa, and Chumpivilca.

This colonising policy served more than one purpose. Its most obvious effect was to secure the quiet and prosperity of recently annexed provinces. It also led to the increased well-being and comfort of the whole people, by the exchange of products. *Mitimaes* in the coast valleys sent up cotton, aji, and fruits to their former homes, and received maize, potatoes, or wool in exchange. The *mitimaes* in the eastern forests sent up supplies of coca, and of bamboos and chonta wood for making weapons, and received provisions of all kinds. This system of exchanges was carried on by means of *chasquis* or couriers, constantly running over excellent roads. A third important end secured by the system of *mitimaes* was the introduction of one language to be used throughout the whole empire, a result which followed slowly and surely. The *Runa-simi*, or one general language, was an immense help in facilitating the efficient working of a rather complicated system of government.

The Inca organisation was not a creation by a succession of able princes. Such a result would be impossible in the course of only a few generations. The Incas found the system of village communities prevailing among the tribes they conquered, and made as little alteration as was compatible with the requirements of a great empire. Their merit as statesmen is that they saw the wisdom of avoiding great changes, and of adapting existing institutions to the new requirements. They did this with a skill and ability which has seldom been approached, and with a success which has never been equalled. Their system was necessarily complicated, but it was adjusted with such skill and ingenuity that it worked without friction and almost automatically, even when the guiding head was gone. An instance of this is recorded by Cieza de Leon, a soldier of the Spanish conquest. One of the details of the system was that when any calamity overtook a particular district, there was another neighbouring district told off to bring succour and supply its proportion of new inhabitants. Cieza de Leon testified that he saw this arrangement actually at work. When the Spaniards massacred inhabitants, burnt dwellings, and destroyed crops in one district of the Jauja valley, he saw the right people come from the right district to succour the sufferers, and help to rebuild the dwellings and re-sow the crops.

The Incarial system of government bears some general resemblance to a very beneficent form of Eastern despotism such as may have prevailed when Jamshid ruled over Iran. There was the same scheme of dividing the crops between the cultivator and the State, the same patriarchal care for the general welfare; but while the rule of Jamshid was a legend, that of the Incas was an historical fact. The Incarial government finds a closer affinity in the theories of modern socialists; and it seems certain that, under the very peculiar condition of Peru when the Incas ruled, the dreams of Utopians and socialists became realities for a time, being the single instance of such realisation in the world's history.

The condition of the people under the Incas, though one of tutelage and dependence, at the same time secured a large amount of material comfort and happiness. The inhabitants of the Andean region of Peru and of the southern half of the coast valleys were practically one people. Slightly built, with oval faces, aquiline, but not prominent noses, dark eyes, and straight black hair, the Inca Indian had a well-proportioned figure, well-developed muscular limbs, and was capable of enduring great fatigue. He was very industrious, intelligent, and affectionate among his own relations; at the same time he was fond of festivity, and of indulgence in drinking bouts. The *puric*, with his family about him, went joyfully to his field work. Idleness was unknown, but labour was enlivened by sowing and harvest songs, while the shepherd-boys played on their *pincullu*, or flutes, as they tended the flocks on the lofty pastures. Wool was supplied to the people for their clothing, and hides for their *usutas*, or sandals, and even some luxuries, such as coca, reached them through the continuous ebb and flow of commercial exchanges by the *mitimaes*. Periodical festivities broke the monotony of work, some of a religious character, others in celebration of family events. The *rutu-chicu* was a festival when a child attained the age of one year and received a name. Others came round when a boy or girl ceased to be nursed. This event was called *huarachicu* for a boy, and *quicuchicu* for a girl. The greatest festival of the year was at harvest time, when the *puric* hung the fertile stalks of maize on the branches of trees, and his family sang and danced the *ayrihua* beneath them. The people were taught to worship the sun and the heavenly bodies, but the chief trust of the labouring classes was in their *conopas* or household gods, representing, as they believed, the essential essences of all that they depended upon for their well-being—their llamas, their maize, or their potatoes. These they prayed to fervently, not forgetting the *huacas* or idols of which there were some in every district, and above all never neglecting the ceremonial burial of llama idols, with small offerings, in the fields, to propitiate the good earth deity.

A proof of the general well-being of the people is the large and increasing population. The *andeneria* or steps of terraced cultivation extending up the sides of the mountains in all parts of Peru, and now abandoned, are silent witnesses of the former prosperity of the country. The people were nourished and well cared for, and they multiplied exceedingly. In the wildest and most inaccessible valleys, in the lofty *punas* surrounded by snowy heights, in the dense forests, and in the sand-girt valleys of the coast, the eye of the central power was ever upon them, and the never-failing brain, beneficent though inexorable, provided for all their wants, gathered in their tribute, and selected their children for the various occupations required by the State, according to their several aptitudes.

This was indeed socialism such as dreamers in past ages have conceived, and unpractical theorists now talk about. It existed once because the essential conditions were combined in a way which is never likely to occur again. These are an inexorable despotism, absolute exemption from outside interference of any kind, a very peculiar and remarkable people in an early stage of civilisation, and an extraordinary combination of skilful statesmanship.

It was destroyed by the Spanish conquest, and the world will never see its like again. A few of the destroyers, only a very few, could appreciate the fabric they had pulled down, its beauty and symmetry, and its perfect adaptation to its environment. But no one could rebuild it. The most enlightened among the destroyers were the lawyers who were sent out to attempt some sort of reconstruction—men like

Ondegardo, Matienza, and Santillan. But they could only think hopelessly what Santillan wrote: 'There was much in their rule which was so good as to deserve praise and be even worthy of imitation.' There were even some faint attempts at imitation, but they failed utterly, and the unequalled fabric disappeared for ever.

NOTE TO THE CHAPTER ON THE CONDITION OF THE PEOPLE

Writers on Peruvian civilisation from the time of Robertson and Prescott have assumed that the whole fabric was originated and matured by the Incas, constructed, as it were, out of chaos. But a more recent school of thinkers has seen the impossibility of such a creation, and holds that the Incas systematised tribal and social organisations which had existed from remote antiquity, and did not create them.

A very able review of the works of those writers who have adopted the opinion that the Incas did not create a system, but adapted one which had long been in existence, was published at Lima in 1908—'El Peru antiguo y los modernos sociologos.' The author, Victor Andres Belaunde, is thoroughly master of his subject. He first explains the conclusions of the German sociologist Cunow, in his 'Organisation of the Empire of the Incas—Investigations into their Ancient Agrarian Communism.' According to Cunow there had existed, from remote antiquity, separate groups organised on the same base as the village communities of India, and the German mark. These were the *ayllus*. He holds that the *ayllus*, as village communities, existed before the empire of the Incas. The Incas respected this *ayllu* organisation, and all they did was to systematise it. Belaunde holds that this hypothesis has caused a complete revolution in the manner of considering the rule of the Incas. The communistic organisation did not originate in the constitution of the Inca monarchy, but was anterior to it. Communism was not here the result of a special political organisation, nor the realisation of a plan of state socialism. It was simply the result of the union of the numerous *ayllus* , who thus. collectively held the land under the domination of the most powerful among them. So that Peru is not the prototype of a paternal monarchy. Communism was not imposed by the Incas. It was not a system conceived by them, and brought into practice by means of conquests and clever alliances. Ancient Peru was not the archetype of socialism, but a vast agglomeration of village communities. After the publication of Cunow's work there appeared 'The Evolution of Political Doctrines and Beliefs' by the Belgian sociologist William de Greef, who devotes an interesting chapter to Peru. His view is practically the same as that of Cunow.

Belaunde then explains the views of two eminent South American writers, Don Bautista Saavedra, a Bolivian, and Don José de la Riva Aguero, a Peruvian.

Saavedra in his work 'El Ayllu' also holds that the *ayllus*, as communities, existed before the rise of the Inca empire. Riva Aguero describes the gradual aggregation of the constituent tribes.

Belaunde proceeds to discuss the views of Prescott, Lorente, Letourneau, Wiener, D'Orbigny, Desjardins, Spencer, and Bandelier, and of the present writer in his essay written for Winsor's narrative and critical history of America. The earlier writers have not attempted to discuss the condition of things previous to the rise of the Incas, and Spencer's theories respecting Peruvian civilisation, in his great work on sociology, are based on misconceptions and inaccurate information.

The present writer, in the course of his studies, was gradually approaching the discovery that Peruvian socialism was not a conception of the Incas, but the result of much more ancient organisations recognised and adopted by the Incas. As will be seen from the present chapter, he has practically come to the same conclusions as Cunow and others who are in agreement with him, which are so admirably summed up by Belaunde in his extremely interesting and able review. But at the same time he does not consider that this pre-existence of communities holding land in common at all detracts from the admiration that is due to the government of the Incas. The wisdom which led the Incas to respect the institutions of the various tribes brought under their rule, and the skill with which they adapted those institutions to the requirements of a great empire, are evidences of no ordinary statesmanship. Their wise policy explains the rapidity of the rise of their empire, and the slight resistance to it.

CHAPTER XII.TTAHUA-NTIN-SUYU

I.Cunti-suyu

THE official name of the Empire of the Incas was *Ttahua-ntin-suyu*, the word *ttahua* meaning four, *ntin* a collective plural, and *suyu* province. 'The four combined provinces,' with reference to the dominions west, north, south, and east of the central land of the Incas. The western division was called *Cunti-suyu*, and included the country from the Apurimac to the maritime cordillera and the coast. *Chinchay-suyu* was the northern division including Huamanca, the valley of the Jauja, Haunuco, Caxamarca, as far as Quito, with the coast valleys. The *Colla-suyu*, or southern division, was the basin of Lake Titicaca, and Charcas, as far as Tucuman, Chile, and the valleys of Arequipa, Moquegua, and Tacna. The country to the east of the land of the Incas and all that was known of the Amazonian forests was *Anti-suyu*.

From a geographical point of view the *Cunti-suyu* division is formed of three regions west of the Apurimac, within the meridians of 70 and 76 W., all watered by tributaries of the Apurimac. The first lies between the Apurimac and the Pachachaca rivers, the second between the Pachachaca and the Pampas, and the third includes the maritime cordillera between those meridians. They may be called, after their chief *ayllus* or tribes, the Quichua, Chanca, and Lucana regions.

The Quichuas occupied the beautiful valley of Apancay, and some valleys in the mountains as far as the fortress of Curamba, beyond the Pachachaca. Their position is partly defined in the account of Tupac's first campaign, when he occupied the Quichua strongholds of Tuyara, Cayara, and Curampa. The Quichuas were very closely allied to the Inca people in race, and their language was the same. Indeed, the first Spanish grammarian of the general language of the Incas called it Quichua, probably from having studied it in their country. Mossi gives a definition of the word from the passive participle of *quehuini* (I twist), which is *quehuisca* (twisted) and *ichu* (grass), that is *quehuisca-ychu* (twisted grass), by syncope *quichua*. It came to mean a temperate region, neither too hot nor too cold.

The Apancay valley presents scenes of great beauty. On the mountain to the south the products of almost every clime may be seen at one glance. The rapid little river flows along at its base, amongst waving maize crops and fruit trees. On the steep slopes immediately above there are crops of potatoes and other edible roots, then pastures on the steep mountain side with rocks cropping out, and higher the peaks shooting up into the sky. On the other side of Apancay there are terraced slopes, and cultivated tracts sloping down to the banks of the Pachachaca. Higher up the Pachachaca and other tributaries of the Apurimac, the mountain gorges and lofty *punas* were inhabited by four *ayllus* of hardy mountaineers closely allied to the Quichuas. These were the *Chumpi-uilcas, Cotapampas, Umasayus,* and *Aymaras.*

The beauty of the scenery between the rivers Pachachaca and Pampas is most striking as the summit ridges are reached, and the eye ranges over such valleys and gorges as are presented by Angamos, Pincos, and Huancarama. On a grassy plateau, commanding the road, is the ancient fortress of Curamba, a stronghold of the Quichuas. It consists of three terraces, one above the other with stone revetments, and a ramp on the east side forming a sloping way to each terrace. There were no doubt stockaded defences when it was used for operations of war. The great feature of this Chanca region is the extensive and fertile valley of Andahuaylas, capable of sustaining a very large population. There are other fertile valleys between Andahuaylas and the river Pampas which, like the Apurimac, flows through a gorge so profound that the vegetation on the river banks is quite tropical.

Beyond the Pampas, in the valleys formed by its tributaries flowing from the maritime cordillera, and on the Pacific slopes, there dwelt two powerful mountain tribes called Soras and Lucanas. They seem to have been more advanced in civilisation than their neighbours, for there are ruins of important edifices in the Sora country, called Vilcashuaman. This was a palace of the Incas and their principal station in Cunti-suyu, but it existed before the annexation, for Montesinos mentions a king of Vilcas, and the Soras did not submit without making some resistance. Their neighbours, the Lucanas, occupied both slopes of the cordillera. On the Pacific side there is a large alpine lake frequented by flamingoes called *Parihuana-cocha*, round the banks of which their principal seat appears to have been. Below is the lovely coast valley of *Nasca*, owing its fertility to the most remarkable system of irrigation in Peru, which I believe to have been due to the skill, intelligence, and industry of the Lucanas. These mountaineers were remarkable for their strength, as well as for their skill and industry. In later times it was their special privilege to carry the imperial litter.

The Nasca valley is one of the most striking monuments of Andean civilisation. The fertilising water is led from the mountains of Lucanas by subterraneous channels, built of stone and the height of a man. Their origin in the mountains is now unknown. The water flows down them perennially, and is eventually spread over the valley by smaller channels, converting a coast desert into an earthly paradise. Pottery of a peculiar design, and believed to be of great antiquity, has recently been found in the valley of Nasca.

II.Chinchay-suyu

Chinchay-suyu, the northern division of the empire, includes the two great ranges of the Andes, and the rich and fertile valleys between them. The direction becomes nearly north and south, following the trend of the coast, not east and west as in Cunti-suyu. The valleys supported very large populations, and the mountains were inhabited by tribes of hardy mountaineers.

When the Inca Pachacuti sent the first army for the conquest of Chinchay-suyu, it included a large contingent of the conquered Chancas, led by one of their own chiefs named Anco-ayllu. They fought well for the Incas, but their leader chafed at his subjection, and incited his men to desert. A plot was arranged, and on a day settled beforehand the Chanca contingent left the camp and, led by Anco-ayllu, they proceeded by forced marches into the Amazonian forests. This exodus was commenced at a place called Huarac-tampu, near Huanuco. They were soon beyond the reach of pursuit, and it is believed that they settled in valleys along the lower course of the Huallaga. They were found there by a Spanish expedition in 1556, and a recent traveller has suggested that the half-civilised Lamistas, or Motilones, on the Huallaga, are their descendants. This event made a deep impression on the Inca recorders, for it is mentioned by several Spanish writers who received their information from the native Amautas.

On marching north from Vilcas-huaman, after crossing the deep gorge of the Pampas by a bridge of aloe cables, the Inca army entered upon the basin of the Jauja river, another tributary of the Apurimac. The various streams flowing to the Jauja are in the bottoms of deep ravines, while the intervening higher lands are fertile and produced large crops. To the west the splendid maritime cordillera rises abruptly, and in this part the fierce and warlike Morochucos sought for pastures and raised edible roots among the giddy heights. To the east were the equally imposing mountains of Cuntur-cunca, in the rear of which the Iquichanos defied invasion. The intervening plains and ravines were inhabited by the numerous tribe of Pocras, who made a desperate fight for independence.

The final stand of the Pocras and Morochucos was on a slope between two ravines, at the foot of the Cuntur-cunca heights. There was a terrible slaughter, and the place was ever afterwards called the AYACUCHO, or 'corner of death.' The remnant of Morochucos fled westward to their own mountains, followed closely by the Inca general, who finally encamped on a grassy slope at the foot of the first steep ascent. As he sat with his officers around him at their evening meal, a falcon soared in circles round his head. He threw up a piece of llama flesh to it, crying out 'HUAMAN-CA' ('take it, falcon!') The tradition was never forgotten, and the natives tell it to this day. The place, afterwards the site of a Spanish city, was called HUAMANCA (Guamanga), in memory of the Inca's supper guest.

Advancing northwards up the Jauja valley, the Incas next defeated and brought under subjection the Huanca nation, which cultivated and inhabited that fertile region. In the mountains to the westward there were two remarkable tribes, the Yauyos and Huarochiris, who appear to have descended into the adjacent coast valleys, and to have greatly increased their well-being by exchanges of products raised in different climes. The Yauyos seem to have spread over the valleys of Pisco, Chincha, Huarcu (Cañete), and Mala; and in a ravine leading up from the Huarcu valley, called Runa-huana, there are some interesting ruins, referred to in an appendix. According to Garcilasso the inhabitants of Huarcu made a very desperate resistance to the Inca arms, and this seems to be confirmed by the fact that the ruins of an extensive Incarial fortress and palace, called Hervay, exist on a defensive hill close to the sea, flanked by a rapid river on one side and the desert on the other.

The Yauyos spoke a peculiar dialect of their own, called *Cauqui*. Much reduced in numbers and living in small villages high up in the mountains, there are now not more than 1500 people who still speak this dialect. Like the Rucanas and Morochucos, the Yauyos are an intelligent race, and make excellent artificers when any of them have opportunities of learning trades in the coast valleys which once belonged to them.

The Huarochiris lived in lofty gorges of the maritime cordilleras to the north of the Yauyos, with terrible passes over the snowy heights. But the descent on either side gradually led down to fairer scenes, on one side to the fertile vale of the Jauja, on the other to the coast valleys of Chilca, Lurin, and Rimac. The imposing grandeur of some of this scenery, contrasted with the peaceful beauty of the rest, seems to have been impressed on the imaginations of the Huarochiri, and to have given rise to a mythology full of quaint legends and fables. These will be discussed in the essay on the religious beliefs of the coast people. The temple to the fish god at Pachacamac attracted pilgrims from far and near as a famous oracle, as well as the oracle which gave its name to the Rimac valley. Both appear to have been due to the highly imaginative tendencies of those of the Huarochiris who settled on the coast. It was a little further north, at Pativilca, on the coast, that the more northern dominions of the Grand Chimu found its southern frontier. But this coast region, between Pativilca and the Rimac, seems to have been long in an unsettled state. The dwellings of the chiefs who occupied the Rimac valley were built on immense mounds of great extent, and strongly fortified. The mountain tribes of the maritime cordillera are quite exceptionally interesting, because the advances they had made in civilisation were due largely to their occupation of valleys on the coast.

The Incas received the submission of the mountaineers without invading their fastnesses, and pressed onwards in their northern conquests. They were now an immense distance from their base, but their generalship was carefully thought out and so sound that they advanced with confidence to the great lake of Chinchay-cocha and the mountain knot of Cerro Pasco, which, like that of Vilcañota, connects the eastern Andes with the maritime cordillera. The march, be it remembered, was not a matter of months, but of years.

The conquerors now entered another region, the basin of the Marañon, and the very remarkable formation known as the 'Callejon de Huaras.' At Huanuco a great palace was projected and afterwards built by Tupac Inca Yupanqui, forming eventually the chief seat of Inca government in Chinchay-suyu. Among the Conchucos they met with a people who had made marked progress in the arts, and had taken their own line in the conception of a religious belief. The Incas passed on and, after slight opposition, occupied Caxamarca. In another campaign Tupac Inca conquered the Paltas, and the turbulent tribe of Cañaris, while the territories of the great Chimu, in the coast valleys, were reduced to subjection. Quito also became part of the empire after one decisive battle.

The greatest proof of the genius of these Inca generals is the way in which they changed their tactics and methods of warfare as soon as they encountered circumstances of which they had previously no experience. Tupac Inca was at the palace he had caused to be built at Tumipampa, in the country of the Cañaris, when he heard of the riches of Manta, the land of emeralds, and of other coast regions. He resolved to explore, and to add these countries to the empire. He led his army down through the dense forests to the country of the Chonos (the modern Guayaquil), constructing a road as he advanced. With a hostile country, difficulties in arranging for supplies, and the extraordinary obstacles caused by the dense vegetation, the enterprise seemed almost hopeless. On reaching the banks of the Guayaquil, where it is navigable, he found the enemy in a large fleet of canoes, while he was without any means of attacking. But with Tupac Inca there was no such word as impossible. Having a very excellent system of road-making, and efficient commissariat arrangements, he was without anxiety about supplies. The more insuperable appeared the difficulties the more determined he was to overcome them. He proceeded to build canoes, and to exercise his soldiers as canoe-men until they were fairly expert. This occupied several months. He then attacked the enemy's fleet, and the manoeuvres continued for several days, sometimes one side and sometimes the other having command of the river. The Incarial soldiers were more accustomed to the use of the lance than to naval warfare, so their very able general gave orders to grapple and fight at close quarters. The result was then no longer doubtful, and the Chonos submitted. The Inca landed where now stands the city of Guayaquil, and after a sojourn of a year he resolved upon the conquest of the island of Puna, in the Gulf of Guayaquil, assisted by the chiefs of the Chonos, who had become his allies. Many canoes were got ready, and good pilots were engaged. Here seamanlike skill was needed rather than reliance upon numbers. But nothing could resist Tupac's superior strategy, and the island was conquered. Most generous terms were granted, and a cordial friendship, cemented by a marriage, was established between the Inca and the Puna chiefs. The coast provinces of Manta and Esmeraldas, to the north, sent in their submission, and the port of Tumbez, to the south of the Gulf of Guayaquil, was fixed upon as a military station.

While the Tupac Inca Yupanqui was at Tumbez, he received information that, far out in the ocean, there were islands called HAHUA-CHUMPI and NINA-CHUMPI, the outer and the fire islands. The Inca was a man of lofty ideals, and, as Sarmiento says, 'he resolved to challenge a happy fortune, and try if it would favour him by sea.' This was a wonderful expedition, but Sarmiento's account is corroborated by Balboa, and I have come to the conclusion that the story of the voyage is historically true.

The Incas caused an immense number of balsas to be constructed, consisting of inflated seal-skins fastened together, and some rafts. He then embarked with a large detachment of his army, leaving the main body to await his return at Tumbez.

Tupac Inca sailed away on this memorable voyage of discovery, disappearing below the horizon of those who gazed from the hills round Tumbez. To them it must have seemed an enterprise as appalling as it was unprecedented. If the Inca ever returned, his people would be convinced that there was nothing he might not do. It is said that he reached the islands, and that he was absent for nine months. Sarmiento believed that he reached the Solomon Islands, but there can be little doubt that it was two of the Galapagos Islands that the Inca discovered and explored. Sarmiento says that he brought back gold, a chair of brass, and the skin and jawbone of a horse, which were preserved in the fortress at Cuzco. It is more likely that the nature of these curiosities was not understood, and that they were really specimens of the large terrapins and other products of the Galapagos Islands.

The conquest and settlement of Chinchay-suyu by the Incas must be looked upon as the greatest of their military achievements. It occupied several years, and there were a number of campaigns. Still, when the immense distances from their base, the care and forethought needed to keep the army properly supplied, the inaccessible character of a great part of the country, and the necessity for adapting the troops to very different kinds of warfare, often in the face of the enemy, are considered, it must 'be acknowledged that the genius and ability of this remarkable race is very striking. The voyage of discovery to the Galapagos Islands is marvellous. These statesmen and warriors were .no ordinary conquerors, and they were well fitted to rule the vast empire they brought together with such extraordinary skill and determination.

III.Colla-suyu

The basin of Lake Titicaca, the land of the mysterious megalithic city, was briefly described in the first essay. After the disruption of the ancient empire there was a long period of centuries of barbarism. The tribes which came to inhabit the country round the lake may have been partly descendants of subjects of the megalithic kings and partly descendants of invaders. They were a hardy race of mountaineers, strong and thick-set, and capable of enduring great fatigue. Like the Incas and Quichuas, they spoke dialects of the same original language.

Of these tribes the CANAS were on the crest of the water-parting between the Titicaca drainage and the Vilcamayu. The COLLAS occupied the whole of the northern half of the Titicaca basin. They were the most numerous and powerful of the tribes in the Titicaca region. Along the western shores of the lake were the LUPACAS. The PACASAS occupied the eastern side, and to the south were the PACAJES and QUILLAGUAS. There was also an almost amphibious tribe living among the reeds in the south-west angle of Lake Titicaca, called URUS. They spoke a language of their own. Another, language, called Puquina, was spoken in part of Colla-suyu. Great invasions from the south are recorded, even from Chile, and the tribes of the lake basin were practised in mountain fighting.

The Collas had acquired predominance over the other tribes, and early writers give the generic name of Collas to them all. It was probably a confederacy, with the Colla chief at its head. He was becoming very powerful, extending his sway over Arequipa and Tacna towards the Pacific, and into some of the eastern valleys where coca is grown. His chief seat was at Hatun-colla, a few miles north-west of the north-western angle of Lake Titicaca. Here there are figures carved on stones, and some few other vestiges of the former greatness of the Colla chief. Just above are the towers or *chulpas* of Sillustani, overlooking a mountain lake.

The Collas buried their dead in cromlechs consisting of huge blocks of stone, many of which are still extant. Later they built circular towers of fine ashlar masonry, vaulted above with a coping round the upper part. Some are square. The best examples are at Sillustani, near Hatun-colla, the probable burial-place of the Colla chiefs.

Chuchi Ccapac was the name of the great chief who haughtily refused to submit to the Inca. He had a large force of hardy mountaineers around him, inured to hardships, brave, and of fine physique. They were concentrated for the defence of Hatun-colla, led by Chuchi Ccapac and all the chiefs of his confederacy.

The Collas were constantly making incursions down the valley of the Vilcamayu, and were as constantly driven back over the pass. At last the Inca built a wall from the snows of Vilcañota across the road to the snows on the western side. The Collas agreed that this should be their boundary. But they broke the treaty and continued their raids. The Inca, therefore, resolved to conquer them. Lizarraga says that the remains of the wall were still visible in his time, at the point on the summit of the pass called La Raya by the Spaniards.

The Inca Pachacuti assembled a great army, crossed the pass of Vilcañota, and advanced across the Collao without opposition until he came in sight of the enemy's forces drawn up in front of Hatun-colla. The proud chief was called upon either to serve and obey the Inca or to try his fortunes in battle. The reply was that Chuchi Ccapac expected the Inca to submit to him, like the chiefs of other nations he had conquered. The answer concluded with a savage threat.

The two armies then encountered each other in desperate hand-to-hand combats, and the issue was for a long time doubtful. The Inca was in every part, giving orders, fighting, and animating his troops. For a moment there was a pause. The slightest thing might have turned the scale. At this momentous crisis the Inca shouted a few words of encouragement and dashed into the thickest of the fight, closely followed by his Orejones. With renewed vigour all his troops rallied, and at length the gallant enemy turned and fled. Chuchi Ccapac was taken prisoner, and Pachacuti entered Hatuncolla in triumph. There he remained until all the confederate tribes were reduced to submission. An Inca viceroy was appointed to govern the Collao, with the necessary garrisons, and Pachacuti returned to Cuzco.

Colla-suyu was not, however, to be subdued in one campaign. A few years afterwards the sons of Chuchi Ccapac escaped, and raised the standard of revolt. The confederate tribes rallied round them. This time the battle took place further north, and the Collas were again defeated with great slaughter, near Lampa. Pachacuti returned to Cuzco, but two of his very able sons, Tupac Ayar Manco and Apu Paucar Usnu, remained to pacify the country, and to extend the conquest southwards over the countries of the Charcas and Chichas.

After the accession of Inca Tupac Yupanqui, the Collas rebelled once more to secure their freedom. They had constructed four strong places, all in the Colla country, to the north of Lake Titicaca, at Llallahua, Asillo, Arapa (on a small lake), and Pucara, an isolated rocky mountain rising out of the plain to a great height. The Inca generals were occupied for several years in reducing these fortresses. The final stand was at Pucara, where the Collas sustained a crushing defeat. All thoughts of further resistance were abandoned.

The Inca proceeded to include Tucuman and Chile in his conquests. A story is told by Montesinos respecting the Chilian annexation which seems quite probable.

It appears that two Chilian chiefs, who had come with a contingent to help the Collas, were taken prisoners and sent to Cuzco. They were received with great kindness by the Inca, who gave them two *Pallas*, his half-sisters, for their wives. They returned to Chile, and had two sons by the Inca princesses. In course of time the Inca's Chilian nephews proposed a visit to their imperial uncle, and arrived at Cuzco with a large retinue. They were received by the Inca with much love and great rejoicings. They entreated their uncle to visit their country, where all desired to see him. He consented to do so in the following year, and his nephews returned to Chile with many Orejones and several Amautas to teach them the art of government. But a number of Chilian chiefs thought that this friendship with the Inca boded no good to them, and they took up arms. The nephews, however, defeated them, even before the Inca could arrive in Chile, which he did with a great army. All the chiefs submitted to him and, after two years, he left his nephews in peaceful possession as his viceroys. His dominions extended to the river Maulé in the south of Chile. Thus the empire was more than 2000 miles in length, from the river Maulé to Pasto.

From that time the Collas and Chilians furnished valuable contingents to the Inca armies.

The Inca Tupac Yupanqui saw the necessity for establishing permanent tranquillity in the Collao by a system of colonisation. Great numbers of Collas and Lupacas were sent to colonise the charming valleys of Arequipa, Moquegua, and Tacna on the west side of the maritime cordillera. Others were sent down into the Amazonian valleys to the eastward, to cultivate coca and wash for gold. Traditions are preserved even now, which tell from which district in the Collao the exiles were taken, and whither sent. The conquest of the Collao was of immense importance, because it was the only source of tin for their bronze weapons and tools, and the principal source of gold from Caravaya.

Tupac Inca was deeply impressed by the vast ruins at Tiahuanacu, of unknown origin, by the beauties of the great lake, and of the sun rising over the snowy peaks of Illimani and Illampu. He caused a palace to be built on the island of Coati, in the lake, with baths and gardens. A number of Orejones remained in the Collao to carry on the administration, and emigrants arrived to take the plac.es of the exiled Collas and Lupacas.

These emigrants were chiefly Quichuas of various tribes from Cunti-suyu. A number of Aymaras, from the headwaters of the Pachachaca, were settled among the remaining Lupacas at Juli on the west coast of the lake, where the languages of the two races appear to have got considerably mixed. In 1576 the Jesuits settled at Juli, and had a printing-press there, and here they learnt the language of the Lupacas from the Aymara emigrants, who gave them many Quichua words, for they seem to have used words of both languages in their conversations. This explains the reason why the first priests who acquired the Colla language and afterwards the Jesuits gave the name of 'Aymara' to the language of the Collao. Ludovico Bertonio was at Juli from 1590 to 1612, and before he arrived the Jesuits had adopted the name of 'Aymara' to what Bertonio calls *esta lengua Lupaca*. He published his 'Arte y Gramatica' of 'Aymara' at Rome in 1603, and a second edition, with a dictionary, at Juli in July 1612. Torres Rubio followed with a grammar and vocabulary of 'Aymara' in 1616. The word 'Aymara' is now generally, but very erroneously, applied to the language and people of the basin of Lake Titicaca.

IV. Anti-suyu

The chain of the eastern Andes is penetrated by five great rivers, which unite to form the 'mighty Orellana.' They flow northwards until they unite, and then flow eastward in one majestic stream to the Atlantic. The Amazonian basin which they traverse consists of millions of square miles of virgin forest. The first river is the Marañon, and being the most western and distant its source in the Andean lake of Lauricocha is considered to be the source of the Amazon. Next is the river Huallaga, flowing north until it joins the Marañon. Further to the east the great Ucayali tributary is formed by the Perene, Apurimac, and Vilcamayu, which all force a way through the Andes. Further south the Tono, Arasa, Inambari, Tambopata, and Beni rise on the eastern slopes of the Andes and do not penetrate the range. With the Mamoré and Itenez they form the great Madeira tributary. The rivers which have part of their courses within the Andean system, all have formidable rapids when they force their way through the mountains and enter the great Amazonian plains. These mountain rapids were called *puncu*, or doors, which the rivers had opened by their irresistible force. That of the Marañon is called the Puncu de Manseriche. On the Huallaga the rapid is known as the Salto de Aguirre, respecting which there is an interesting tradition: then the river is navigable for 160 miles. The Ucayali, a broad stream navigable for 1400 miles, breaks through the mountains at Canchaguayo. The Vilcamayu, navigable for 100 miles, enters the primeval forests by the Puncu de Mainique.

The vast Amazonian forests are approached by the descent of the eastern side of the Andes, down gorges and ravines which present magnificent scenery, the long spurs being covered with the richest tropical vegetation to their summits. Here are seen the lovely chinchona trees with their red-veined glossy leaves, and panicles of white flowers with pink laciniae, emitting a delicious fragrance. Here, too, are many species of Melastomas, especially the Lasiandra with its purple flowers and triple-veined leaves. But the flowering trees and bushes are innumerable, and above the thick foliage are seen the feathery fronds of palm trees. From the loftier mountains waterfalls may be seen in rapid descent until they are lost to view behind the dense vegetation; some in sheets of spray, others like films of lace, but most in a solid volume of moving water, all glittering when the clouds open and the sun throws its rays upon them. These are scenes of unsurpassed loveliness. But in the plains below the view is obstructed by the vegetation growing in dense masses beneath the lofty trees. Only on the river banks there are beautiful views formed by long vistas of tropical vegetation.

It was to the forests eastward of Cuzco that the Incas first turned their attention. To the east of the valley of the Vilcamayu the range of the Andes is cut laterally by the Yanatilde valley, and further east by the long valley through which the river Paucartampu flows. Both the Yanatilde and Paucartampu flow north to join the Vilcamayu, though their previously unknown courses were only traced, for the first time, a very few years ago. From the last range of the Andes, on the east side of the Paucartampu river, the descent is rapid into the *montaña*, as the tropical forests are called by the Spaniards. The forests were very scantily inhabited by wild Indians who wandered about, some in canoes as fishermen, some hunting with bows and arrows or the *pucuna* (blowpipe). A few had some affinity with the people of the Andes, but the great majority of the Amazonian tribes were of a different race.

The subjugation of the parts of the *montaña* nearest to the foot of the Andes was a matter of great importance to the Incas. In the tropical valleys the coca plantations were formed and every Peruvian chewed coca. From the *montaña* also came supplies of bamboo, of wood of the chonta palm for their weapons, other timber for building, plumes for head-dresses, and the principal supplies of gold.

The campaign of Tupac Inca Yupanqui for the conquest of Anti-suyu was, like all his warlike operations, masterly in design and bold in execution. The long valley of Paucartambo, at the foot of the last ridge of the Andes, formed a convenient base where the three columns, forming the army of Anti-suyu, was to assemble. The Inca himself started from a place in the valley called Ahua-tuna, descending into the forest by the lovely ravine of the Chiri-mayu. The central column under Prince Uturuncu Achachi, the Inca's brother, was at a place called Amaru, the modern town of Paucartampu. It was to enter by the route now called 'Tres Cruces.' A captain named Chalco Yupanqui led the right column from the Pilcopata or 'garland hill.' At the same time the *montaña* of Marcapata, to the south, was to be invaded by Apuccurimachi with a fourth column.

The three columns in the Paucartambo valley were to start at the same time on converging lines, to form a junction at Opotari in the forest, about twelve miles from the foot of the mountains. The inhabitants, who belonged to the tribe called Campas or Antis, submitted at once, and the settlement called Abisca, for the cultivation of coca, was formed near the river Tono. The Inca then began to make a road through the dense forest in order to reach the settlements of the next tribe. Tall trees were climbed to seek out the positions of inhabited places by the smoke rising over the trees. The troops suffered from the change of climate, and from the toil of hewing out the road. There was much sickness and many died. At one time the Inca, with a third of the troops, lost his way and wandered about for many days until, at last, they fell in with the column of Uturuncu, who put them on the route. The combined forces then descended the river Tono.

The final result of the campaign was that three branches of the Campas, a tribe of fine muscular men and beautiful women, submitted and became subjects of the Inca. These were the Opataris, the Mañaris, called also Yana-simis or 'black mouths,' and the Chunchos. The submission included a vast tract of forest, yielding valuable timber, and with land suitable for coca plantations. The Mañaris were also met with on the lower reaches of the river Vilcamayu, and in the *montaña* beyond the Vilcapampa mountains, and they always remained friendly to the Incas. Further north there was a fierce and hostile tribe called Pilcosones.

The Marcapata column led by Apu-ccuri-machi marched eastward to the Inambari, and advanced as far as a river called Paytiti, where their leader set up the frontier pillars of the Inca. Uturuncu was left to complete the conquest, aided by detachments of colonists who made clearings for coca plantations, and collected chonta poles and other products. Most of the settlements were round Abisca, and in the basin of the river Tono; but there were others on the banks of the Vilcamayu and in Marcapata.

After the conquest of Colla-suyu the forests of the province of Caravaya also became a great source of wealth to the Incas. Large numbers of Collas were sent down into the beautiful valleys to grow fruit trees and cultivate the coca plant, as well as to work and wash for gold. Indeed, it was principally from Caravaya that the immense quantities of gold came which were used for vases and other utensils, for adorning the temples and idols, for the imperial thrones and litters, for ornamenting the rich dresses, and for many other purposes. Much gold also came from the rich valleys whose rivers unite to form the Beni.

Further south there were some fierce and savage tribes in the forests of the 'Gran Chacu,' or great hunting ground. Among these the most troublesome were the Chirihuanas, who were said to have been cannibals. They were always hostile, and even had the audacity to make incursions into the higher lands of Charcas.

On the river Huallaga the remnant of the Chancas took refuge, and the ancestors of the existing Amazonian tribe of Mayorunas are said to have fled before the Chancas to settle lower down the course of the great river. The present Huallaga tribes of Cholones and Motilones, or Lamistas, may be descendants of the Chancas. The Incas occupied Chachapoyas in the basin of the Marañon. An expedition is recorded, sent by the Inca Huayna Ccapac to the country of the Cofanes, a tribe in the forests of the river Napo to the east of Quito. A story is also told by Montesinos of some Orejones having found their way thence by the waterways and through the dense forests to Cuzco, a voyage which occupied several years. It was certainly a most remarkable achievement if true, and considering the energy and intelligence of these people I can see no sufficient reason for doubting the truth of the story.

The wisdom of the Incas is well shown in their policy with regard to the region of Amazonian forests. They made no useless raids or expeditions, but worked with the distinct object of securing advantages for the empire. From their *montaña* settlements, quite sufficiently supplied with labour, they received gold in large quantities, coca which was almost a necessary of life for their people, timber for building, wood of the chonta palm for lances and other weapons, bamboos, plumes of feathers, fruit, and medicinal herbs, gums, and resins. In return the colonists received meat and potatoes, maize, clothing, salt and other condiments. The forests of the *montaña* formed a part, and no unimportant part, of the great system of Incarial administration.

CHAPTER XIII. THE COAST VALLEYS

THE coast of Peru was a late conquest of the Incas. It contained distinct civilisations, that to the north, especially, presenting historical and philological problems as yet unsolved. Its physical aspects are unique and extremely interesting. They demand attention before considering the little that is known of the ancient people inhabiting this wonderful region in ages long past.

A strip of land, averaging a width of from 20 to 60 miles, extends from 4 to 20 S. or upwards of 1500 miles between the maritime cordillera and the Pacific Ocean. It has been upraised from the sea at no very remote period. The same shells as exist in the present ocean are mingled with the remains of man. Corn-cobs and cotton twine were found by Darwin at a height of 85 feet above the sea. This upheaval must have taken place at a time not only when man was occupying the land, but when there already existed an agricultural community raising maize and cotton crops.

The Peruvian coast is practically a rainless region, and the reason for this phenomenon attracted the attention of most of the early writers. Acosta is very hazy on the subject. Cieza de Leon comes nearer the true cause, which is of course due to the height of the Andes. For the southeast trade-wind blows obliquely across the Atlantic Ocean until it reaches the coast of Brazil, heavily laden with moisture. It continues to carry this moisture across the continent, depositing it as it proceeds, and filling the tributaries and sources of the Amazon and La Plata. Eventually this trade-wind reaches the snow-capped mountains of the Andes, and the last particle of moisture is wrung from it that the very low temperature can extract. Meeting with no evaporating surface and with no temperature colder than that to which it was subjected on the mountain tops, the trade wind reaches the Pacific Ocean before it again becomes charged with fresh moisture. The last drop it has to spare is deposited as snow on the tops of the mountains. It reaches the coast region as a perfectly dry wind.

Yet the coast atmosphere is not absolutely dry. There is intense heat and a clear sky from November to April, but in May the scene changes. A thin mist arises which increases in density until October, rising in the morning and dispersing at about 3 P.M. It becomes fine drizzling rain called *garua*. This *garua* extends from the seashore to near the mountains, where rain commences, the line between the *garua* and the rain region being distinctly marked. There are even estates where one half the land is watered by *garuas*, the other half by rain. But the prevailing aspect of the coast is a rainless desert traversed, at intervals, by fertile valleys.

The climate of the coast is modified and made warmer by another agency. Not only is the constantly prevailing wind from the south, there is also a cold current always flowing with a temperature several degrees lower than that of the surrounding ocean. It is believed by some to be derived from the Antarctic regions, by others that it is formed by cold water in the depths rising to the surface. Be this how it may, the Humboldt current, as it has been called since 1802, profoundly affects the climate of the Peruvian coast, which is cooler and drier than any other tropical region.

Although the greater part of the coast region consists of desert or of arid and stony ranges of hills, it is watered by rivers which cross the desert at intervals and form fertile valleys of varying width. The deserts between the river valleys vary in extent, the largest being upwards of seventy miles across. On their western margin steep cliffs rise from the sea, above which is the desert plateau, apparently quite bare of vegetation. The surface is generally hard, but on some of the deserts there are great accumulations of drifting sea sand. This sand forms isolated hillocks, called *medanos*, in the shape of a crescent, beautifully symmetrical, with sharp ridges, and their convex sides turned towards the trade-wind. Any stone or dead mule forms a nucleus for them; but they are constantly shifting, and a strong wind causes an immense cloud of sand, rising to a hundred feet and whirling in all directions. When at rest the *medanos* vary in height from eight to twenty feet, with a sharp crest, the inner side perpendicular and the outer with a steep slope. Scattered over the arid wilderness they form intricate labyrinths, and many a benighted traveller has lost his way among them and perished with his mule, after wandering for days. Such unfortunates form nuclei for new *medanos*. At early dawn there are musical sounds in the desert. They are caused by the eddying of grains of sand in the heated atmosphere on the sharp crests of the *medanos*.

Apparently the coast deserts of Peru are destitute of all vegetation. As far as the eye can reach there is a desolate waste. Yet two or three kinds of plants do exist. The smaller *medanos* are capped with snowy white patches, contrasting with the greyish white which is the colour of the sand. This whiteness is caused by innumerable short cylindrical spikes of an amaranth. Its stems originate in the ground beneath the *medano*, ramify through it, and go on growing so as to maintain their heads just above the mass of sand. The two other herbs of the desert are species of *yuca* which form edible roots, but maintain a subterranean existence for years, only producing leafy stems in the rare seasons when moisture penetrates to their roots. Near the foot of the mountains are the tall branched cacti. When the mists set in, the *lomas*, or chains of hillocks, near the coast undergo a complete change. As if by a stroke of magic blooming vegetation overspreads the ground, which is covered with pasture and wild flowers, chiefly composites and crucifers. But this only lasts for a short time. Generally the deserts present a desolate aspect, with no sign of vegetation or of a living creature. In the very loftiest regions of the air the majestic condor may perhaps be seen floating lazily, the only appearance of life.

Imagine the traveller, who has wearily toiled over many leagues of this wild and forbidding region, suddenly reaching the verge of one of the river valleys. The change is magical. He sees at his feet a broad expanse covered with perpetual verdure. Rows and clumps of palms and rows of willows show the lines of the watercourses. All round are fruit gardens, fields of maize and cotton, while woods of *algaroba* fringe the valley and form one of its special features.

The *algaroba* (*Prosopis horrida*) is a prickly tree rarely exceeding forty feet in height, with rugged bark and bipinnate foliage. The trunks never grow straight, soon become fairly thick, and as their roots take little hold of the friable earth, they fall over into a reclining posture, and immediately begin to send off new roots in every part of the trunk in contact with the soil. They thus assume a twisted and fantastic appearance, more like gigantic corkscrews than trees. The *algaroba* has racemes of small yellowish green flowers which nourish multitudes of small flies and beetles, and they in their turn supply food to flocks of birds, most of them songsters. The flowers are followed by pendulous pods, six to eight inches long, containing several thin seeds immersed in a mucilaginous spongy substance which is the nutritive part. The timber is very hard and durable, and also makes excellent firewood. With the *algaroba* there are bushes, sometimes growing into trees, of *vichaya* (*Capparis crotonoides*), a tree called *zapote del perro* (*Colicodendrum scabridum*), and an *Apocynea*, with bright green lanceolate leaves, and clusters of small white flowers. Near the roots of the cordillera the vegetation becomes more dense and varied.

The fertile valleys of the coast vary in extent and in the supply of water they receive. Some rivers have their sources beyond the maritime range, and the flow is abundant and perennial. Others are less well supplied. Others, with sources in the maritime cordillera, are sometimes dry, and the supply of water is precarious.

Altogether there are forty-four coast valleys along the 1400 miles of Peruvian sea-board, and, with reference to the study of the former history of the country, they may be divided into three sections. The twenty northern valleys include the territory of the Grand Chimu, whose history is still shrouded in mystery. The central twelve formed the dominions of the Chincha confederacy, and the southern twelve were only peopled by *mitimaes* in later times, though there was a scanty aboriginal fishing population.

Valleys of the Chimu	Valleys of the Chincha confederacy	Valleys in the south
1 Tumbez	21 Chancay	33 Acari
2 Chira	22 Carabayllo	34 Atequipa
3 Piura	23 Rimac	35 Atico Yauca
4 Motupe or Leche	24 Lurin	36 Ocoña
5 Lambayeque	25 Mala	37 Majes
6 Eten	26 Huarcu	38 Vitor
7 Saña	27 Tupara	39 Tambopalla
8 Pacasmayu	28 Chincha	40 Ylo
9 Chicama	29 Pisco	41 Locumba
10 Muchi	30 Yca	42 Sama
11 Viru	31 Rio Grande	43 Tacna
12 Chao	32 Nasca	44 Azapa
13 Santa		
14 Nepeña		
Pativilca		
15 Casma		
16 Culebra		
17 Huarmay		
18 Parmunca		
19 Huaman		
20 Huara		
Supe		

CHAPTER XIV. THE CHIMU

ONE of the most difficult problems in the study of the American races is the origin and history of the civilised people in the northern coast valleys of Peru. Here we find ruins of vast extent with evidence of artistic skill and somewhat florid taste, systems of irrigation on a gigantic scale and planned with marvellous skill, every square foot of ground carefully cultivated. Writing of the Chira to the north, Mr. Spruce says that there are ancient aqueducts all the way down the valley from near its source. Water is conducted across ravines and along the faces of steep declivities. There was also provision for collecting rain water in the *años de aguas* by canals along the base of the Mancora hills and cliffs of the valleys, and for storing it in reservoirs made by throwing strong dikes across the outlets of ravines. The whole valley was then under cultivation with a dense population, proved by the *middings* sometimes miles in extent, strewn with fragments of shells and pottery. The richly embossed walls, the gold and silver work, the astonishing versatility in the infinite variety of their pottery, and the patterns of their cotton cloths, all point to a race which had reached a high state of civilisation. A grammar, composed by a descendant of one of Pizarro's followers over a century after the Spanish conquest, has preserved some knowledge of their otherwise lost language, but of their history we know absolutely nothing. We only learn from the Spanish historians of the Incas that the sovereign of the coast people, called by them the Grand Chimu, was subdued by the Incas about four generations before the Spaniards came, and that he possessed great riches. Nothing more. There is only one tradition preserved, and that does not refer to the Chimu, but to his feudatories in the Lambayeque valley.

The kernel of the Chimu problem is in the ruins between the Spanish town of Truxillo and the shores of the Pacific Ocean. Here the Chicama and Muchi rivers combine to form a wide extent of cultivable land, which is situated in the centre of the northern coast valleys, having eight on the north and eight on the south side of it. The vast extent of the ruins shows that this was the centre of the Chimu's power. The people were perhaps known to themselves as Muchoen, from the river which supplied water to their capital, or possibly Nofoen, their word for a man. Their language was Muchica.

The great Chimu ruins were first described, in any detail, by Don Mariano E. Rivero in his 'Antiguedades Peruanas,' then by Squier, and more recently by the French traveller Wiener. Of these accounts that of Squier's is the most accurate and intelligent. It must be understood that, owing to the elaborate and complicated arrangement of rooms, passages and enclosures, and to the destruction that has taken place in the search for treasure, an intelligible description, even with plans, is exceedingly difficult.

We may picture to ourselves a vast fertile plain, at least ninety miles long from south to north, watered by the three rivers Chicama, Mansiche, and Viru, and bounded on one side by the Andes and on the other by the Pacific Ocean. In the centre, but bordering on the seashore, was the great city of the Chimu, surrounded by highly cultivated land sustaining a dense population. An effective system of irrigation was essential for the cultivation of this extensive area and for the existence of the people in the city. An aqueduct took off the water of the Muchi river high up among the mountains. It was carried across the valley on a lofty embankment of stones and earth sixty feet in height, the channel being lined with stones. On the slope overlooking the ruined city the water is distributed through smaller channels over the plain, and into the numerous reservoirs in the city. A lofty wall of great thickness extended for miles along the eastern or inland borders of the city, and within it were extensive gardens each with its irrigating channel.

The ruins of this unique city now consist of labyrinths of walls forming great enclosures, each containing many buildings, with here and there gigantic mounds. These mounds or pyramids are the most marvellous features of the ruins. The *huaca* or mound called 'Obispo' by the Spaniards is built of stones, rubble, and adobes, covers an area of 500 square feet, and is 150 feet high. Another was called 'Toledo,' in which great treasure was found. The excavator, Garcia de Toledo, in 1577, dug out gold to the amount of 278,174 *castellanos de oro*, of which 61,622 were paid as the royal fifths. Excavations were continued at intervals. In 1797 the treasure called *Peje chico* was secured. The *Peje grande* has yet to be found. Altogether millions have been obtained in gold ornaments or bars. The mounds are honeycombed with passages leading to store-houses or sepulchral chambers.

The great mounds presented a very different appearance in the time of the Chimu. Originally they were in terraces, on which buildings were erected with pitched roofs, and tastefully painted walls. Verandahs, supported by the twisted stems of algaroba trees, afforded shade, and there were communications with the interior passages and chambers. From the seashore these structures, with gardens at their bases, must have presented a magnificent effect.

The principal palace has been well described by Squier. Imagine a great hall 100 feet long by 52½ wide, with walls covered with an intricate series of arabesques, consisting of stucco patterns in relief on a smooth surface. The walls contain a series of niches with the arabesque work running up between. The end wall is pierced by a door leading to corridors and passages in the pyramidal mounds. One corridor leads to a place where there was a furnace for metallurgic work, near a walled-up closet full of vessels and utensils of gold and silver.

There is a low, broad mound at a distance of a hundred yards from the palace, which has been excavated and proved to be a cemetery. There were mummies in niches elaborately clothed and plumed, with gold and silver ornaments on the dresses of fine cotton cloth. The patterns, woven into the cloth and coloured, are birds striking the heads of lizards or seizing fish. In the centre there is a structure sixteen feet square and twelve high, with entrances at each end, leading to a space ten feet by five, with a series of platforms on either side. Here, no doubt, the funeral rites were performed.

The two most remarkable structures among the ruins are called palaces by Rivero, and factories by Squier. They are surrounded by exterior walls of adobes on foundations of stone and clay, five feet thick and thirty in height. One factory is 500 yards by 400. An entrance leads to an open square with a reservoir in the centre, faced with stone, sixty feet long by forty. Round the square there are twenty-two recesses, probably shops opening upon it, and at one end a terrace with three rooms leading from it. This square, with its reservoir, appears to have been the market-place. There are six minor courts, and streets or passages with many rooms opening upon them. Of these rooms there are no less than 111, with walls twelve feet high and high-pitched roofs. The objects of these extraordinary buildings were very puzzling. They were certainly not palaces, as Rivero supposed. Squier's conjecture is no doubt the correct one. They were busy factories, hives of industry. Here were the workers in gold, silver and bronze, the designers, the dyers, the potters, and the weavers. It must have taken many generations, nay centuries, for these busy modellers and designers to reach the high standard displayed in their best metal and clay work, and in their cotton fabrics.

The most frequent ornaments are fish, lizards, serpents, a long-legged bird, a bird devouring a fish. The ornament of the head-dress of chiefs was like an inverted leather-cutter's knife, as Squier describes it, with plumes, and diadems of gold and silver. The golden cups and vases were very thin, with the ornaments and figures struck from the inside. Gold ornaments on the dresses were also frequent. Mr. Spruce describes a series of plates, almost like a lady's muslin collar in size and shape, covered with figures. On one of them there were nearly a hundred figures of pelicans. Every figure represents the bird in a different attitude, and, as they have been stamped, not engraved, a separate die must have been used for each figure. Silver vases and cups were of various shapes, sometimes modelled into the form of a man's head. Silver lizards, fishes, and serpents were sewn on the dresses as ornamental borders.

The most astonishing work of the northern coast people was their modelling and painting in clay. The prevailing colours of their vases were white, black, and a pale red, the designs being painted, in various colours, on a white ground. A great number are double, some quadruple, and a prevailing feature is the double spout. It is not too much to say that not only the fauna and flora of the coast, but also the manners and customs of the people, are depicted or modelled on their vases. There are met with various kinds of fruits and vegetables, shells, fish, lizards, deer, monkeys, parrots and other birds, and a sea-lion with a fish in its mouth. In short, there are countless varieties of forms and combinations, hardly two specimens alike. By far the most interesting are the human heads. Some are almost majestic, and are evidently portraits. Others show the face distorted in pain, others smiling or singing, some with a rapt expression as in a trance. There are also figures playing on musical instruments, others spinning. Some vases represent a human hand, others a foot showing how sandals were worn. Architecture, the arts, customs, and religious ideas are depicted. Squier describes one scene of a chief seated in the verandah of a house with a high-pitched roof, raised on four terraces. The chief has a plumed head-dress, a lance in one hand and a drinking-cup in the other. A long procession is approaching, with persons singing and playing on cymbals, tambourines, Pandean-pipes, and trumpets of clay. Another vase has a foot-race painted round it. There is another showing a combat between a serpent-warrior and a crab-warrior, perhaps a legend of a contest between land and sea. There is a vase with winged figures, and another very remarkable one, in the British Museum, of a winged warrior in the act of flying.

Another very striking group of Chimu works of art are the silver models cast in a single piece. Squier mentions a man and woman in a forest, the trees being like algarobas; also a child in a hammock swinging between two trees, and a serpent crawling up one, below a kettle by a fire of sticks. These can only have been intended as ornaments for rooms, but it is a mystery how they can have been cast without wax. Doubtless there was a substitute of some kind.

Warlike implements were lances, darts, and cktbs fitted with bronze stars. Warriors carried an oblong shield of thick matting. Vast numbers of tools and agricultural implements in bronze have been found. There are chisels of various sizes with sockets for handles, hoes curved and flat, and knives.

Their textile fabrics were very fine and marked in a variety of patterns, for the coast people cultivated an indigenous cotton, the staple of which is unequalled for length combined with strength. Occasionally the cotton plants produced a boll of a rich nankin colour which was specially valued. The weavers had various dyes for the patterns on their fabrics, and produced tunics and cloaks of great fineness and beauty, often almost covered with thin gold and silver plates, with borders of blue and yellow feathers.

We conclude from the ruins of their buildings, their works of art, and the vast treasure that has been found, that the Chimu kept a court of extraordinary magnificence, and that his subjects, though working hard, lived in abundance and comfort.

There is only one account of the religion of these people, written by Antonio de la Calancha, in his 'Coronica Moralizada del Orden de San Agustin.' Calancha was prior of the Augustines at Truxillo in 1619, eighty years after the Spanish conquest, when traditions still lingered among the people. He says that the Chimu worshipped the moon, called *Si*, as the principal god, because it ruled the elements and caused the tempests. The temple of the moon was called *Si An*. They held that the moon was more powerful than the sun because the latter did not appear in the night, while the moon appears both by day and night. Sacrifices were offered to the moon, consisting, on great occasions, of children wrapped in coloured cloths, with chicha and fruits. Devotion was also shown to some of the stars. The ocean, called *Ni*, received worship and, apparently, sacrifices; as well as the earth, *Vis*. Prayers were offered up to one for fish, and to the other for good harvests, with offerings of flour of white maize. Certain rocks were also objects of veneration, called *Alespong*.

The *Si An*, or temple of the moon, was to the south, near the banks of the river Muchi. It is a rectangular structure, 800 feet by 470, covering seven acres, with a height of 200 feet. It is built of large adobes. It consists of a level area 400 feet by 350, and 100 feet above the plain, beyond which rises a pyramid of nine stages or terraces, 200 feet square. On the other side of the pyramid, which is the highest part, there is a platform 80 feet lower, and another lower still. The mass of adobes is probably solid. Here were performed the great religious ceremonies. The gorgeous processions issued from the palace and proceeded to the temple of the moon. There were the musicians with their instruments, the minstrels and singers, the warriors with their long lances and plumed head-dresses showing distinctive ranks, the priests and courtiers, and the Chimu himself in his litter, wearing the jewelled diadem and clothed in robes of fine cotton covered with gold plates, and bordered with fringes of bright-coloured feathers.

Calancha tells us that the physicians, called *Oquetlupuc*, effected their cures with herbs, and were much venerated, but their punishment, when a patient died owing to their neglect or ignorance, was death. He gives us no details respecting their cemeteries and methods of sepulture, although this is a most important point. Like the Incas, the Chimus thought it a sacred duty to preserve the bodies of the deceased as mummies, and to bury with them their most valued possessions. To this practice we owe the discovery of so many hundreds of specimens of their beautiful works of art. Quite recently Mr. Myring has discovered a great cemetery at the foot of the mountains above the Chicama valley, and has brought to England a magnificent collection of pottery and of gold and silver ornaments. The islands off the coast, called Guañape and Macabi, were looked upon as sacred cemeteries, and had been so used for more than a thousand years. Besides pottery and other works of art, numerous mummies have been found at various depths, all females, and all headless. It would seem that they were the victims of sacrifices in remote times.

Cemeteries have been found in all parts of the coast. There are also very interesting ruins in the valleys to the south of Truxillo, all of the same character, and imposing irrigation works. Squier describes a vast reservoir in a lateral valley among the hills, whence water was supplied to the fields of the Nepeña valley. This reservoir was three-quarters of a mile long and half a mile wide, with a massive stone dam across the gorge, eighty feet thick at the base, between the rocky hills. The reservoir was supplied by two channels, one starting fourteen miles up the gorge, the other coming from springs five miles distant. There were houses in the valleys with richly painted walls raised on terraces, verandahs covered with passion-flower plants yielding refreshing fruit, gardens and cultivated land extending to the seashore, dark algaroba woods, and a background of snowy mountains. All this leaves an impression of luxury bordering on effeminacy, but it is qualified by the very numerous representations, on their pottery, of warriors armed to the teeth. It is true that some of the things that are modelled in clay give a low idea of the moral character of the people.

The language, called MOCHICA by Bishop Oré, has been preserved in a grammar and vocabularies, though as a spoken tongue it has long been extinct. We are indebted to the priest, Fernando de la Carrera, for the grammar. He was a great-grandson of one of the Spanish conquerors, Pedro Gonzalez de la Carrera, and was brought up at Lambayeque, where he learnt the language in his childhood. It is so excessively difficult, especially the pronunciation, that no grown-up person could learn it. Fernando de la Carrera eventually became cura of Eeque, near Chiclayo, and here he composed his grammar, calling the language YUNCA, which is the Quichua name for the people of the coast, the MOCHICA of Oré. It was printed at Lima in 1644, and is very rare. There is a copy in the British Museum which belonged to Ternaux Compans. William Humboldt had a manuscript copy made, which is at Berlin. There is one copy in Peru, belonging to Dr. Villar, for which he gave £25. We are, therefore, deeply indebted to Dr. Gonzalez de la Rosa for having recently edited a reprint. Dr. Middendorf has also translated and edited Carrera's grammar, adding several vocabularies and words collected at Eten. It was in this little coast village, where the people were famous for their manufacture of straw hats, that the Mochica language lingered down to recent times.

There was another language in the northern coast valleys, which Calancha calls *Sec.* In 1863 Mr. Spruce collected thirty-seven words of this language, then still spoken at Golan, Sechura, and Catacaos. They have not the remotest resemblance to equivalent words in the Mochica, Chibcha, or Atacama languages.

The Mochica language is entirely different from Quichua, both as regards words and grammatical construction. It has three declensions depending on the termination of the noun in a consonant, two consonants, or a vowel. The adjective precedes the substantive, and the pronouns precede the verb. The roots of the tenses remain unaltered, the conjugating being effected by pronouns, and the passive voice by the verbs substantive, of which there are two. Prepositions come after the noun. The vocabulary is fairly abundant, and there is a sufficiency of nouns and verbs for the expression of abstract ideas.

We know nothing of the origin of the Chimu and his people. Not the vestige of a tradition has come down to us. All their designs and ornaments refer to their environment. There is nothing which points to a foreign origin. Their civilisation appears to have been developed by themselves without outside contact, in the course of many centuries. Yet the temple of the moon on the Muchi river, and the great pyramids, remind us of similar Maya works. If there was communication it was by sea, and at some very remote period. There is one coast tradition referring not to the Chimu, but to one of his feudatories, the chief of Lambayeque, to the north. It is related by Miguel Cavello Balboa in his work entitled 'Miscelanea Austral.' This cavalier, after serving as a soldier in the French wars, became an ecclesiastic, and went to South

America in 1566. He wrote his work, apparently at Quito, between 1576 and 1586.

Balboa tells us that, a long time ago, a great fleet of boats came from the north under the command of a very able and valiant chief named *Naymlap*, with his wife *Ceterni*. The emigration may have been from the coast called by the Spaniards Esmeraldas, or from further north. Naymlap was accompanied by eight officers of his household: his purveyor, *Fongasigde*; his cook, *Ochocalo*; his trumpeter and singer, *Pitazofi* and *Ningentue*; his litter bearer, *Ninacolla*; his perfumer, *Xam*; his bath man *Ollopcopoc*; and *Llapchilulli*, his worker in feathers. The chief landed at the mouth of a river called *Faquisllanga*, where he built a temple called *Chot*, in which he placed an idol he had brought with him, made of a green stone, and called *Llampallec*, whence the name of Lambayeque. Naymlap died after a long reign, and was succeeded by his son *Cium*, married to a lady named *Zolzdoñi*. After a long reign Cium shut himself up in an underground vault to die and conceal his death from the people, who thought him immortal. A list of eight other kings is given, the last of the dynasty being *Tempellec*. This unfortunate prince wanted to take the idol out of Chot when an unheard-of thing happened. It began to rain, and the deluge continued for a month, followed by a year of sterility and famine. The priests, knowing of the conduct of Tempellec with regard to Chot, looked upon him as the cause of the calamity. So they put him into the sea, with his feet and wrists tied. Lambayeque submitted to the Chimu, with the other valleys ruled by descendants of Naymlap. Llapchilulli, the feather worker to Naymlap, was a favourite of that chief, who gave him the valley of Jayanca, where his descendants reigned for several generations.

Soon after the extinction of the Naymlap dynasty the Inca invasions began. Authorities differ. Garcilasso de la Vega says that the Inca army advanced along the coast from the south, with a large contingent of allies. Each valley was desperately defended, yet the army of the Chimu was obliged to retreat fighting, and at length the great chief was forced to submit. Sarmiento makes the Inca army descend from the mountains round Caxamarca, subdue the Chimu, and carry off treasure to a vast amount. Balboa tells us that the Incas had many conflicts with the Chimu, but that the details are forgotten. We learn from Montesinos that the Incas finally prevailed over the Chimu by cutting off his water supply. It is certain that the Chimu submitted. He was visited by the Inca Huayna Ccapac, large numbers of artisans were sent to Cuzco, and a military road was made over the valleys and deserts of the coast. This was about four generations before the arrival of the Spaniards, when Cieza de Leon saw and described the Inca roads and buildings. In the height of their power the Chimu must have had considerable trade. Wool and metals came from the mountains; chonta, palm wood, bamboo, parrots, monkeys and other animals from the eastern forests; emeralds and other precious commodities from the northern coast.

The valleys to the north submitted to the Inca without any contest, except from the Penachis, a savage tribe living on the flanks of the mountains. The chief of Jayanca was suspected of complicity with them, and was sent a prisoner to Cuzco, where he lingered for many years. At length his son obtained his release, but he died on the way back. The body was embalmed and sent to Jayanca. The chief of Lambayeque, named *Esquen Pisan*, was summoned to Cuzco by the Inca Huascar. He went willingly, because he was in love with a young lady of the coast, who was a maid of honour to the widow of Huayna Ccapac. Her name was *Chestan Xecfuin*. The young chief of Lambayeque sought for his love and found her. They were united and, on their way back, she gave birth to a son, who received the name of *Cuzco Chumpi*.

Then the Spaniards under Pizarro appeared on the scene, leaving Tumbez on their march southwards on May 16, 1532. Pizarro came to the river Chira at Amotape, where he burnt two chiefs and some other Indians. He founded his town of San Miguel at Tangarara, on the Chira river, afterwards removed to Piura. He was at Pocheos, Zaran in the Piura valley, Copiz and Motupe, eventually reaching Cinto in the valley of the river Leche. Xecfuin Pisan, the chief of Lambayeque, wished to submit to what appeared inevitable, but the people were infuriated.

They burnt down his house, and he perished in the flames. His son Cuzco Chumpi submitted, and was baptised with the name of Pedro. We hear also of his son, Don Martin Farro Chumpi. Pizarro rested at La Mamada in the valley of Jequetepeque, and marched thence up the mountains to Caxamarca, which place he reached on November 15, 1532. In 1535 the conqueror was again in these coast valleys. He founded the city of Truxillo, named after his old home in Spain, close to the city of the Chimu in 8 6′ S., and Balboa tells us that Pizarro was much struck by the grandeur and beauty of the edifices constructed by the ancient kings. But he came as a fell destroyer. The cruelty of the Spaniards extinguished the ancient Chimu civilisation before even a few years had passed. Cieza de Leon tells us of the rapid depopulation of the valleys, and in his time vast tracts were becoming waste for want of people to cultivate the land. The census of the Piura valley alone, made by order of Dr. Loaysa, the first Archbishop of Lima, showed a population of 193,000 Indians. In 1785 it was 44,497, and these chiefly negroes. The race is now practically extinct. The brilliant conceptions, the masterly execution, the untiring industry, the wealth and magnificence, all passed away and are forgotten.

Yet the story of the coast civilisation of the Chimu is worthy of being rehabilitated. There should be a thorough examination and study of the Mochica language; an exhaustive classification of Chimu works of art in public museums and private collections; a knowledge of all the authorities; and scientific plans of all the ruins. From the works of art alone a fairly complete idea may be obtained of the conditions of life, the manners and customs, even the legends and religious ideas of the extinct people. The result would be the rehabilitation of an ancient people whose history would be quite as interesting, and in some respects even more curious, than the histories of the Aztecs of Mexico, or the Chibchas of Bogota.

CHAPTER XV. THE CHINCHA CONFEDERACY

THE territory of the Chimu ended to the south at Paramunca, in 10 51′ S. The coast thence to latitude about 15 S. includes the perennially watered valleys of Huara, Chancay, Caravayllo, Rimac, Lurin, Mala, Huarcu, Chincha, Pisco, Yca, Rio Grande, comprising five valleys converging into one, and Nasca, with deserts between them. There are also a few inhabited valleys with watercourses coming from outside the region of regular rains, such as Chilca and Asia. The irrigated valleys supported a dense population in ancient times, the chiefs of each valley being independent, though acting together as a confederacy for certain purposes.

There are reasons for the conclusion that these more southern valleys had also been inhabited from a very remote period. On the island of San Lorenzo, opposite to the mouth of the Rimac, Darwin found the same shells as occur in the ocean at the present time, at a height of 85 feet, and with them the evidence of man's existence, including cobs of Indian corn and cotton twine. The depth at which ancient relics have been found in the deposits of guano on the Chincha Islands has been considered as another proof of the very remote period when there were inhabitants in these coast valleys. There is, however, some reason to doubt the cogency of this argument. Still the evidence, especially that given by Darwin, is in favour of the peopling of these valleys from a very remote antiquity.

Whence, then, did these coast people originally come? I believe that the mountains of the maritime cordillera, with their gorges and ravines opening on the coast valleys, answer the question. In a former chapter we have seen that the mountain fastnesses of Huarochiri, Yauyos, and Lucanas overlook the coast, and were inhabited by hardy tribes of mountaineers speaking a dialect of Quichua. From remote antiquity they descended into the coast valleys and multiplied exceedingly, being periodically recruited from the mountains.

We have no history, barely a tradition, to throw any light on these coast people—nothing but the confused side-light thrown by their ruins and the contents of their tombs. Touching their superstitions and religious beliefs we have a little more, due to the fact that two or three priests, commissioned to extirpate idolatry, prepared interesting reports which have fortunately been preserved.

The former density of the population is shown by the irrigation works, and also by the fact that the ruins of ancient villages are found on the skirts of the mountains and deserts, and not within the valleys, so as to reserve every square foot for cultivation. The chiefs, however, formed their strongholds in the centre of their dominions. These consisted of huge mounds, or *huacas*, as the ruins are now called. In the great valley of the Rimac, where now stand the city of Lima and the seaport of Callao, as well as in the other valleys, there are several of these vast mounds built of large adobes. The interiors were used as places of sepulture. On the platform, raised high above the plain, was the chief's palace, made defensible, whence the cultivated lands could be overlooked and the approach of an enemy discerned. At the foot of these mounds there are the ruins of barracks occupied by the followers and attendants of the chief.

The pottery and other works of art found in the tombs are exceedingly interesting, and show that commercial intercourse existed between the Mochicas and the most southern coast dwellers. The Chimu influence is apparent. The most interesting relics are those brought to our knowledge by Reiss and Stübel in their beautifully illustrated work recording the results of their excavations at Ancon, to the north of Lima. Besides the mummies and pottery, and warlike implements, there were cotton cloths worked in various patterns, the workbaskets of ladies with their sewing and spinning articles, and even dolls and other playthings for children. In the more southern valleys the discoveries of pottery and other relics in the places of sepulture have been very numerous. In the valley of Yca I also found a stone vase with two serpents carved round it. In the Nasca valley, in the far south, a number of specimens of painted pottery have recently been discovered, which are believed to be very ancient. But all are inferior to the Chimu works of art, both in design and workmanship.

Some curious mythological fables, belonging as much to the coast valleys as to the adjacent mountainous province of Huarochiri, have been preserved by Dr. Francisco Avila, the cura of San Damian, in Huarochiri, in 1608. This province of Huarochiri, with its lofty mountain ranges, is drained by the rivers Eimac and Lurin. It appears that the tradition of the people was that in the *Purun-pacha*, or most remote times, the land of Huarochiri was *yunca*, that is to say that it had a climate similar to the coast valleys. The tradition seems to point to a period before the Andes were raised to their present elevation.

These people, who spoke a dialect of Quichua, preserved a tradition, handed down to them from the megalithic age, of the supreme god of Pirua, the 'UIRA-COCHA.' To his name they attached the words 'CCONI-RAYAC,' meaning 'appertaining to heat.' They addressed him as 'Ccoñi-rayac Uira-cocha,' saying, 'Thou art Lord of all; thine are the crops, thine are all the people.'

Yet with all their reverence for the Deity, they told grotesque mythological stories about him. In one of these there was a virgin goddess whom he caused to conceive by dropping before her the fruit from a lucma tree. To her own astonishment the goddess, whose name was Cavillaca, gave birth to a son. She assembled all the *huacas* (gods) to see who was the father, by the test of the child recognising him. Uira-cocha came as a wretched mendicant. The child went at once to the beggar as his father. Cavillaca was ashamed and enraged at being supposed to have connection with any one so despicable. She snatched up the child and fled towards the sea. Uira-cocha resumed his godlike form and, clothed in golden robes, he ran after her. His splendour illuminated the whole country, and he cried to her to turn and look at him, but she rather increased her speed, disdaining to look on such a vile and filthy creature. She was soon out of sight, and when she reached the shore of Pachacamac she entered the sea with her child.

They were turned into two rocky islets, which may still be seen. Uira-cocha continued the pursuit, asking several animals, as he passed them, whether the goddess was near or far off. These were a condor, a skunk, a lion, a fox, a falcon, and a parrot.

The condor said he had seen the goddess pass, and that if Uira-cocha went a little faster he would catch her. So Uira-cocha blessed the condor and promised great powers of flight to all future condors. He then met the skunk, who replied to his question that Cavillaca was far away and that he could never overtake her. So Uira-cocha cursed the skunk, and condemned it to have a strong scent so as to be easily caught. The lion's reply was favourable, so the king of beasts received a blessing. He was to be respected and feared in life, feeding on the llamas of sinners, and after his death his skin, with the head, was to be honoured by being worn by men at great festivals. Uira-cocha next met a fox, who told him that his running was useless. The fox's curse was that he would be hunted during life, and that his skin would be despised after death. The cheering answer of the falcon secured for him a great blessing. He was to breakfast on delicious little birds, and after death festive dancers were to honour his skin by wearing it as a head-dress. Lastly, some parrots gave him bad news, and the curse upon them was that in feeding they should never be safe, for their own cries would betray them.

These talks with the birds and beasts on the road must have delayed the god a good deal, so that when at last he reached the seashore he found that Cavillaca and her child were turned into rocks in the offing. Uira-cocha walked along the seashore until he met two young daughters of the fish god Pachacamac, but they flew away from him in the shape of doves. For this reason their mother, who had gone to visit Cavillaca, now turned to a rock, was called *Urpi-huachac*, or the 'mother of doves.' Uira-cocha was angry, and looked about to see how he could injure her. In those days there were no fishes in the sea. But Urpi-huachac reared some in a pond; so the enraged god emptied all the fish into the sea, and from them all the fishes that are now in the sea were propagated. This tradition was rooted in the hearts of the people, and in Avila's time the condor, falcon, and lion were looked upon as sacred, and were never killed. Avila knew of a condor which lived under the bridge at the village of San Damian for many years after it was too old to fly. The diligent priest has preserved several other mythological legends.

The temple of Pachacamac was dedicated to a fish god, and is alluded to in this legend of Cavillaca. An immense mound of stones and adobes rises to a height of 200 feet, on the right bank of the river Lurin, near the seashore. It stands on the frontier line, with the fertile valley of Lurin on one side and the sandy desert on the other. The temple is built in three wide terraces, with a platform on the summit. The side-walls are supported by buttresses, but the buildings on the terraces and on the platform have been destroyed. The god gave out oracles which attracted many people from great distances. The Incas are said to have consulted it. Hence a large town sprang up to the east of the temple, and the worship of the creator Uira-cocha was superseded by that of the fish god Pachacamac. The site of the temple was very grand and the view was imposing from the platform, with the bright green of the Lurin valley on one side, the desert on the other, and the lofty mountains of Huarochiri in the rear. The view in front, of the Pacific Ocean, with the sun setting behind the rocks which were once Cavillaca and her child, is very grand.

But the fish god and its oracle lost their fame and importance after the conquest by the Incas. It was January 30, 1533, when Hernando Pizarro, and the recorder of his journey, Miguel Astete, reached the temple of Pachacamac. Astete tells us that an idol of wood was found in a good, well-painted building which the people looked upon as their creator and sustainer. Offerings of gold were placed before it, and no one was allowed to enter the temple except the officiating priests. Hernando Pizarro caused the temple to be pulled down and the idol to be broken and burnt before all the people. The Inca, after the conquest of these coast valleys, had built a temple to the sun on the upper platform. But great part of the town was in ruins, and most of the outer wall had fallen, an indication that the fish god and its oracle had lost their importance under the Incas. Astete tells us that the name of the principal chief was Tauri-chumbi. Because this idol was called Pachacamac an erroneous idea has prevailed that the Supreme Being was worshipped at this place. *Pacha* means the earth, and *Camac*, maker or creator. The name was given to their chief idol and oracle, but there is no valid reason for the conjecture that it conveyed any abstract belief in a Supreme Being. On the contrary, the coast people had degraded the primitive and pure religion of megalithic times into a mass of legendary lore, and a system of local image worship combined with divination, soothsaying, and sorcery.

Father Pablo Joseph de Arriaga, a Jesuit, was busily employed, like Avila, in the extirpation of idolatry on the coast and in Conchucos, and his report to the Royal Council of the Indies was published at Lima in 1621. He tells us that each *ayllu* had an idol common to the whole tribe, as well as special idols for families, with sacrificial priests. The people long clung to their custom of preserving the bodies of their relations in rocky or desert places, even taking them from the churchyards, where the curas had ordered them to be buried, in the dead of night. They said that they did this 'cuyaspa,' for the love they had for them. On festivals they assembled by *ayllus*, each one with its mummies, offering to them clothes, plumes, jars, vases, skins of lions and deer, shells and other things. They invoked the ocean as *Mamacocha*, especially those who came down from the mountains, the earth as *Mamapacha* at seed-time, to yield good harvests, the *Puquios* or fountains when water was scarce. Hills and rocks were worshipped and had special names, with a thousand fables about their having once been men who were turned into stones. Many *huacas* (or gods) were of stone carved in the shape of men, women, and animals. All had special names, and there was not a boy in the *ayllu* but knew them. Those which were the guardians of the villages were called *Marcaparac* or *Marcacharac*. Their *Penates* or household gods were called *Conopa* or *Huasi-camayoc*. Large stones in fields called *Chichic* or *Huanca*, and other stones in the irrigating channels; received sacrifices. Then there were the *Saramamas* and *Cocamamas*, or the 'mother,' *i.e.* representative deity of *sara* (maize) and *coca*. Besides the sacrificing priests there were hosts of diviners and soothsayers. Arriaga and his colleague Avendaño boasted of having destroyed 603 *huacas*, 617 *malquis* (mummies), 3418 *conopas*, 189 *huancas*, and 45 *mamasaras*.

The coast people were steeped in superstitious observances, as this report sufficiently proves, but, nevertheless, they were laborious and intelligent, excellent cultivators, good artisans and, above all, admirable contrivers of irrigation works.

The finest example of an effective irrigation system is that enjoyed by the valley of Nasca, which, as has already been stated, was probably peopled by the mountaineers of Lucanas. Here was a tract of country at the foot of the mountains which originally only received a precarious supply of water from the coast range. Practically it was a desert. The Lucanas converted it into a garden. Of all the earthly paradises in which Peru abounds, Nasca is one of the most charming. The two main channels are brought from the mountains by subterraneous tunnels, the origins of which are unknown. They continue right down the valley, and smaller channels branch from them, also subterraneous in their upper courses but coming to the surface lower down. From these secondary channels the water is taken off, in smaller channels, to irrigate the fields and gardens. There were similar works for the great valleys of Rimac, Lurin, Mala, Huarcu (Cañete), Chincha, Pisco, and Yea, but none more complete and scientifically designed than those of the vale of Nasca.

The inhabitants of these coast valleys appear to have had the generic name of Chinchas, from the great valley of Chincha, originally peopled by the mountaineers of Yauyos. They were trained to the use of arms, and had frequent wars with the subjects of the Chimu, perhaps also among themselves. Their conquest by the Incas took place before that of the Chimu. Garcilasso de la Vega tells us that there was desperate resistance in the different valleys, the Chinchas forming a confederacy, and that they were not subdued until after several well-fought campaigns. The name of their principal leader was Cuis-mancu, the chief of the Eimac valley. After they were at length subdued, they joined the Incas as allies in the war against the Chimu.

The Incas erected two important palace-fortresses on the coast. One was on the frontier between the Chinchas and Mochicas, called Paramanca. It was an extension of a more ancient work built by the Chimu, and is described, by both ancient and modern writers, as an edifice of imposing appearance, with painted walls. The other Inca stronghold was on an eminence with precipitous sides, at the mouth of the river now called Cañete. It consisted of two blocks of buildings in the Inca style of architecture, one with a vast hall and passages opening upon one side, leading to small chambers. Between the two blocks of buildings there was an open space, or *place d'armes*, overlooking the plain, with the rapid river washing the base of the height. The place is now called Hervay. It was designed to overawe the great valleys of Huarcu (Cañete) and Chincha.

The coast valleys continued to flourish under the Incas, and their own hereditary chiefs were confirmed as governors under the Inca system. When Hernando Pizarro arrived at Pachacamac, in January 1533, most of these hereditary governors seem to have sent in their submission.

South of Nasca the valleys do not appear to have had either an early history or a dense population. There was an aboriginal race of fishermen called Changos, and the Atacamas far to the south, of whose language a vocabulary has been preserved. These fishing tribes used balsas of inflated sealskins. The southern valleys were eventually peopled by *mitimaes*, or colonists, chiefly from the Collas. Acari, the next valley to Nasca, is mentioned by several early writers, and may, perhaps, be included in the Chincha confederacy. Next came Atequipa, Atico, Ocona, Camana, and Majes. Arequipa, Moquegua, and Tacna, with its port of Arica, were occupied by Colla colonists, but not, apparently, in great numbers or at a very early date.

CHAPTER XVI. THE CATACLYSM

THE overwhelming catastrophe, which destroyed the delicate and complicated organism of Peruvian civilisation, had been preceded by a war of succession. There had been events of this kind before, the last recorded one having preceded the accession of Pachacuti. None had ever been so prolonged and so serious. Yet it is probable that it would not have had any disastrous effect on the general well-being of the empire. It only temporarily affected that section of the community which was told off for military duties. One is reminded of the evidence given by Mr. Thorold Rogers respecting our War of the Roses. The conflict so little affected the daily work of the people and the business transactions of the community that, in all the hundreds of manor accounts over all parts of the country that he had examined during the period, there is not a single allusion to the civil war.

The great Inca Huayna Ccapac left Cuzco on his northern campaign in about the year 1513, and was occupied for twelve years in completing his conquests around and to the north of Quito. At the time of his departure from Cuzco he had had children by four Ccoyas of the royal family, and many others by concubines. The first queen was Mama Cusirimay, the mother of his eldest son, Ninan Cuyuchi. The second and favourite queen was Mama Rahua Ocllo, the mother of Inti Cusi Hualpa, who was surnamed Huascar, from the village near Cuzco where he was born. The third was named Tocta Cuca, a princess of the lineage of Pachacuti, and the mother of Atahualpa. Mama Runtu was the fourth, mother of the princes Manco and Paullu.

On leaving Cuzco the Inca took with him the two Ccoyas Cusirimay and Rahua, his eldest son, Ninan Cuyuchi, and his third son, Atahualpa, both having reached man's estate, besides many other relations and leading councillors. He left a regency at Cuzco consisting of an uncle and a brother, in charge of his sons Huascar, Titu Atauchi, Manco, and Paullu.

The great northern campaign of Huayna Ccapac was admirably conducted, and some very able natives of the Quito province were trained under this great leader, and became distinguished generals, chief among them being Quizquiz, Chalcuchima, and Rumi-ñaui. But the prowess of Atahualpa was not such as to satisfy his father. Meanwhile Huascar was living in luxury at Cuzco. Felicitations and presents were sent to him from the provinces, and among them an exceedingly beautiful maiden arrived from Yca, on the coast, named Chumpillaya, accompanied by her parents.

Huascar fell desperately in love with the coast maiden. She received the surname of 'Curi Coyllur,' or the golden star, and the young Inca had a daughter by her who received the same name. But the jealousy of the other women led to the death of Chumpillaya by poison, and her child was placed under the care of the princess Cahua Ticlla, one of Huascar's sisters. The romantic love story of Curi Coyllur runs like a silver thread through the record of the war of succession.

Huayna Ccapac, the last of the imperial Incas, died at Quito in 1525, after a reign of from thirty to forty years, the last twelve having been completely occupied by his campaigns to the north of Quito. The body was conveyed to Tumi-pampa, where it was embalmed. He had declared his eldest son, Ninan Cuyuchi, to be his heir, but as he was in bad health, Huascar was nominated in the event of his elder brother's death. Ninan Cuyuchi died very soon after his father, and Huascar appears to have been unanimously proclaimed sovereign Inca.

Preparations were then made for the conveyance of the body (*malqui*) and *huauqui* of Huayna Ccapac to Cuzco. His first queen, Cusirimay, had died at Quito. Mama Rahua, therefore, had charge of the body during the long journey, accompanied by some of the Inca's oldest and most trusted friends and councillors, chief among them being Auqui Tupac Yupanqui. Atahualpa excused himself from accompanying the funeral cortege. Speeches have been put into his mouth by one or two Spanish writers. Probably he had reason to be doubtful of his reception by the new Inca. He may have already conceived ambitious schemes, for he found that the Quito generals were devoted to his interests. At first Huascar is said to have given him the title of *Incap Ranti*, or Viceroy in Quito. But if this friendly feeling ever existed, it was of very short continuance.

On the arrival of the Ccoya Mama Rahua and her companions on the plain of Suriti, near Cuzco, with the body of Huayna Ccapac, the news was brought to Huascar that his brother Atahualpa had remained behind. He was furious. Auqui Tupac Yupanqui and his companions were arrested, questioned respecting the absence of Atahualpa, and, as their answers were not considered satisfactory, they were put to death. The Ccoya Mama Rahua was indignant at the execution of her friends, and the friends of her deceased lord. She never forgave her son for these acts of injustice and cruelty. It was long before she would consent to the marriage of her daughter Chuqui Urpay with Huascar, which took place after the obsequies of the great Inca Huayna Ccapac. The widowed queen took up her abode at the village of Siquillapampa, a few miles from Cuzco.

Atahualpa resolved to send an embassy to his brother, with valuable presents, brought by envoys who were instructed to offer his submission and homage. For this delicate mission he selected a handsome and valiant youth named Quilacu Yupanqui, son of the murdered Auqui Tupac Yupanqui. He was accompanied by four older chiefs.

On his arrival at Suriti the envoy received a welcoming message from the queen-dowager, who was fond of young Quilacu. He had been brought up in her palace at Cuzco, and was a foster-brother to her daughter Chuqui Urpay. Mama Rahua invited him to come to Siquillapampa, and to reside there until he received orders as to his reception from the Inca. The old queen sent out a number of beautiful girls to meet her friend Quilacu, and among them was Huascar's daughter, Curi Coyllur, the golden star, the fairest of the fair maidens of Cuzco. During his short residence at Siquillapampa, Quilacu conceived an ardent affection for the beautiful girl, and he had the happiness to find that his love was returned. There was a brief but delightful time under the shade of the molle trees, on lawns carpeted with the *cantut* and *amancay*, where the noise of bubbling fountains mingled with the songs of many birds. Lofty mountains surrounded the little valley, and here all but love was forgotten.

All too soon the spell was broken. An order came for Quilacu and his embassy to proceed at once to Calca, in the vale of Vilcamayu, where the Inca was then residing. The young envoy placed the presents at the feet of Huascar, and assured him of his brother's loyalty. The Inca looked at him with disdain, spurned the presents, and acctised him of being a spy. His four colleagues were put to death, and he was sent to Cuzco to await further orders. An old servant was sent to report his treatment and the murder of his friends to Mama Rahua Ocllo while he remained in suspense. At length Quilacu received his dismissal. He was ordered to return to Atahualpa and to warn him that he would soon have to render an account of his conduct to his sovereign.

A secret message reached Siquillapampa that Quilacu would, if possible, turn off the road and claim Curi Coyllur from her aunt and guardian, the princess Cahua Ticlla. The beautiful girl looked out anxiously for her lover. When she saw a labourer in the far distance with a plough (*taclla*) on his shoulder, she thought it was him. At last a troop of wayfarers was seen, wending their way along the Chinchay-suyu road. Standing under the molle trees, by the side of the waving corn, she saw the travellers disappearing over the crest of the distant hills, and gave way to despair. Suddenly Quilacu rushed out of the maize-field, and in a moment the lovers were locked in each other's arms. They were joined by Cahua Ticlla, to whom Quilacu related all that had taken place at Calca and Cuzco. He asked the princess for the hand of her niece, but she replied that they must wait for more peaceful times. She, however, promised that Curi Coyllur, who was only sixteen, should wait for him for three years. With this he was obliged to be contented, and setting out on his way to Quito, he reported the results of his mission to Atahualpa.

Quilacu was quickly followed by a large army commanded by a general named Atoc, and the forces of the two brothers encountered each other at Ambato, near Quito. Huascar's forces were entirely defeated, the general being captured and put to death. Huascar then sent another army to Tumipampa, under the command of Huanca Auqui, one of the Inca's numerous half-brothers. This unfortunate general seems to have done his best, but he was defeated at Tumipampa, then near Caxamarca, then at Bombon, and was finally driven back into the valley of Jauja. Here he received large reinforcements under another leader, named Mayta Yupanqui, who upbraided the unlucky Huanca Auqui for his defeats. Meanwhile the Inca Huascar celebrated an expiatory fast called *Itu*.

Atahualpa's army was commanded by a savage but very able native of Quito, named Quizquiz, with Chalcuchima as his lieutenant and colleague, while young Quilacu had charge of a reserve force. Three years had nearly expired. The aunt, Cahua Ticlla, was on the point of death, and Huascar threatened to force Curi Coyllur to marry one of his captains. But she was resolved to be true to her lover, and to go in search of him. One night she cut off her long hair, put on the dress of one of her men-servants, and, as the army of Mayta Yupanqui passed by Siquillapampa, she slipped out of the house and mingled with the camp followers.

Quizquiz, having marshalled his forces, advanced against the combined army of Huanca Auqui and Mayta Yupanqui. A desperate battle was fought at a place called Yanamarca, which was long doubtful. One of the wings of Atahualpa's line was hotly pressed, when Quilacu came up with his reserves. This turned the scale. The Incas broke and fled. But Quilacu was severely wounded. He fell among a heap of dead, at a moment when his men were fully occupied in the pursuit of the enemy, so that they did not notice the absence of their leader. The tide of battle rolled onwards and he was left to his fate.

Crushed under the weight of the fallen, and faint from loss of blood, Quilacu was for a long time insensible. When at length he recovered consciousness, he saw a boy traversing the field of battle, appearing to be in search of some one among the disfigured corpses. The wounded chief cried out and succeeded in attracting the boy's attention. He came at once, stanched the wounds, and helped Quilacu to reach the banks of a little stream. Here he collected brushwood, lighted a fire, and gave further aid to the wounded man. Quilacu began to question the lad as to his motive for helping an enemy. His answer was: 'Brother! I am a native of this country. My name is Titu: ask me no more.' Next day Titu led Quilacu to an abandoned hut, where for many weeks he was unconscious with a raging fever, tenderly nursed by the helpful lad.

The Peruvian fugitives rallied at the pass of Ancoyacu, which Mayta Yupanqui proposed to fortify and defend, but Huanca Auqui had lost heart, and they fell back on Vilcas-huaman. The Inca Huascar was now thoroughly alarmed. He consulted the *huacas* and oracles, and was told that if he put himself at the head of his army, leading it in person, he would be victorious. Reinforcements were hurried up from Colla-suyu, and even from Chile, and Huascar found himself at the head of a large army, on the plain of Suriti.

Huanca Auqui, who had fallen back from Vilcas-huaman, was stationed to defend the bridge of the Apurimac. The Chilians were encamped on the heights commanding the valley of Cotabambas, with the Collas and the Charcas contingent. The rest of the army was in the Cotabambas valley. Quizquiz gave up all hope of crossing the profound gorge of the Apurimac in the face of an enemy. He detached Chalcuchima to approach Cuzco by way of Chumpivilcas. He then attacked the main division of Huascar's army, and was repulsed with heavy loss.

What followed is a little obscure. It would seem that the Inca conducted a reconnaissance in force up a ravine opening on to the Cotabambas valley. It was in reality a carefully arranged ambuscade. The Inca was suddenly surrounded, dragged out of his litter, and taken prisoner. When this became known, all resistance ceased, and the Incarial army was dissolved. Atahualpa's generals marched in triumph to the capital, encamping outside at a place called Quisipay. The chiefs of Cuzco and the Inca's mother, Rahua Ocllo, submitted and acknowledged Atahualpa as their sovereign. The old queen even upbraided her son for his injustice and cruelties, and told him that his own wickedness was the cause of his misfortunes. The unhappy prince certainly paid dearly for his sins. All those who were near and dear to him were massacred before his eyes. Then an order came from Atahualpa that his brother Huascar, with his mother and principal councillors, were to be brought to him at Caxamarca.

But the terrible drama was drawing to its astounding close. News came to Cuzco of the arrival of the mighty strangers, then that Atahualpa himself was a prisoner in their hands, next that a ransom in gold was to be paid for his release. Atahualpa had been accepted as Inca after the victories of his generals. The mechanism of the empire went on working as if nothing had happened, and when the orders came for the gold to be sent to Caxamarca, the roads were promptly traversed by the bearers of gold in all shapes and forms. The army of Quizquiz and Chalcuchima evacuated Cuzco, and proceeded towards Caxamarca in some confusion, ready to obey and help their captured sovereign. The atrocities said to have been committed by these conquerors while at Cuzco were naturally exaggerated, the accounts having been received by the Spanish writers from the conquered side. The immediate relations and friends of Huascar were slaughtered, and, for some reason which is not quite clear, the *malqui* of the great Inca Tupac Yupanqui was desecrated and its guardians were put to death. But there was no general massacre of the Incas, and as soon as Cuzco was evacuated by Atahualpa's generals, the Orejones resumed their offices and duties, accepting the young prince Manco as their Inca when the news of Atahualpa's death arrived.

The unhappy Huascar, with his mother and wives and chief officers, were being taken as prisoners to Caxamarca. Pizarro heard of the war waged against each other by the two brothers, and he told Atahualpa that he would judge between them. This threat induced Atahualpa to send an order for the prisoners to be put to death. It reached their guard at Antamarca, where Huascar, his mother and wives, and all his friends, were massacred. One lad escaped, a natural son of Huascar named Huari Titu. He brought the news to Caxamarca, and furnished Pizarro with an excuse for the execution of Atahualpa.

On the death of Atahualpa the gold and silver ceased to arrive. All that was on its way was concealed, but already an amount equivalent to £3,500,000 of our money had reached the Spaniards at Caxamarca, chiefly in the form of square or oblong plates which had been used to adorn the walls of houses. A far greater amount was concealed, and has never yet been found, though the secret has been handed down, and on one occasion a small portion was used in the interests of the people.

The story of the Spanish invasion and civil war has been told in the classic pages of Prescott and Helps, and forms no part of this essay except so far as it concerns the fate of the Incas. The army which vanquished Huascar was scattered, Quizquiz and Chalcuchima were to meet their deserts from men as ruthless and cruel as themselves. The Spaniards were on the march to Cuzco.

Through all these mighty events the boy Titu continued to nurse the wounded chief in the lonely hut. They lived on roots and the milk of llamas. When, after many months, Quilacu became convalescent, Titu began to make excursions with the object of obtaining news. Titu then revealed herself to her lover as Curi Coyllur, who had taken upon herself the disguise which enabled her to escape from a hated marriage, to seek for her beloved, to save his life, and to nurse him through a long illness. She told him that everything was changed, that both Huascar and Atahualpa were dead and their armies dispersed, and that strange men had arrived from the ocean, whose power was irresistible. She went to Jauja, where she fortunately met Hernando de Soto, one of the best of the Spaniards, who had protested against the murder of Atahualpa. He heard her very touching story through an interpreter, and befriended her. He gave clothes to the lovers, and they were baptised with the names of Hernando and Leonor, and happily married.

But Quilacu did not long survive. After his death Curi Coyllur became the mistress of her benefactor. Her daughter, Leonor de Soto, was married at Cuzco to a notary named Carrillo, and had several children.

The empire of the Incas did not fall without more than one gallant effort to save it. Titu Atauchi, one of the sons of the great Inca Huayna Ccapac, was a youth of ability and resource. He was resolved to resist the murderers of his brother, and collected a considerable force with the object of impeding the advance of the Spaniards towards Cuzco. With 8000 men he attacked their rearguard, threw it into confusion at a place called Tocto, in the province of Huayllas, and captured eight prisoners. He took them to Caxamarca, which had been abandoned by the Spaniards. Among these prisoners was Francisco de Chaves of Xeres, one of the most honourable and enlightened of the conquerors, and one of the twelve who protested against the murder of Atahualpa. Among the others were Sancho de Cuellar, Hernando de Haro, and Alonso de Alarcon. Cuellar had been clerk to the court at the mock trial of Atahualpa. He was tried and publicly executed at the same pole against which the Inca was strangled. Alarcon, whose leg was broken, was carefully tended. Chaves and Haro, who had protested against the Inca's execution, were treated with the greatest kindness. The prince Titu Atauchi made a treaty with Chaves to be ratified by Pizarro:

1. The Spaniards and natives to be friends.
2. Prince Manco to be acknowledged as Inca.
3. All the laws of the Incas, in favour of the people, and not opposed to Christianity, to be maintained.

Chaves and his comrades were then set free, with many good wishes, and proceeded to Cuzco. Unfortunately the enlightened prince Titu Atauchi died shortly afterwards.

The Incas and Orejones of Cuzco assembled after the departure of their conquerors, the savage generals of Atahualpa. They were in considerable numbers, for we know from Sarmiento that there were numerous representatives of all the principal *ayllus* at and round Cuzco forty years afterwards. The rightful heir, Prince Manco, was a young lad. His councillors came to the conclusion that the power of the Spaniards was irresistible, but that fair treatment might be secured by submission. Manco, therefore, was taken out in the royal litter, with a large attendance, to meet Pizarro at the bridge of the Apurimac.

The Inca was received very cordially by the Spanish leaders. They escorted him to Cuzco, and the ceremonies of his accession were allowed to be performed with all the usual splendour. Pizarro may have been influenced by Francisco de Chaves and others of that stamp in this wise acceptance of the Inca's rightful position, but it led to no useful result. Pizarro was a man of great natural ability, and very far from having been the worst among the conquerors, only seeking for the gratification of his avarice. He was a statesman of enlarged views, but limited by his ignorance and want of education. He did not in the least realise the value and adaptability of the intricate administrative mechanism he was destroying. Trained lawyers and statesmen came after him, some of whom fully recognised that the Incas were far more able and enlightened governors than their Spanish conquerors, but it was then too late. It is just possible that if such a man as Francisco de Chaves had been in the place of Pizarro, things might have taken a better turn, for the intentions of the councillors in Spain were good; but it is scarcely probable.

As it was, the affairs of Peru went from bad to worse. Pizarro went to found his capital at Lima, his brothers remained at Cuzco, and his colleague Almagro undertook his distant expedition to Chile, accompanied by Prince Paullu, the brother of Manco, and by the Uillac Uma (High Priest of the Sun), another son of the great Inca Huayna Ccapac. Manco, as he advanced in years, found that he was a mere puppet, and that his people were being treated with such cruelty and injustice that they were ready to make an attempt to throw off a yoke which had become unbearable. Manco escaped, and put himself at the head of a great army of Orejones ready to strike one last blow for freedom. The Sacsahuaman fortress was occupied by the patriots, and the Spaniards were closely besieged in the ancient city of the Incas.

The story of the siege of Cuzco has been told by Prescott. It was a final effort. The loss of the fortress deprived the patriots of their last hope. The old Inca chief hurled himself down the precipice rather than surrender. Another such deed is recorded of the old Cantabrian chiefs who died rather than yield to the Romans. Young Manco raised the siege of Cuzco on the approach of Almagro. Marching down the lovely vale of Vilcamayu he made a last stand in the famous stronghold of Ollantay-tampu. Here he repulsed the attack of Hernando Pizarro: the last Peruvian victory.

Forced to evacuate Ollantay-tampu by Almagro's lieutenant, Orgoñez, Manco retreated into the little known mountainous district of Vilcapampa, where the Inca sovereignty was upheld for thirty years longer. Manco's brother Paullu threw in his lot with the Spaniards. Prince Paullu went with Almagro to Chile, and afterwards, joining Vaca de Castro, he was christened as Don Cristoval, and was granted the palace overlooking Cuzco, at the foot of the fortress, called the Colcampata. It had been built by, and was the abode of, the great Inca Pachacuti. At the western end of its façade the little church of San Cristoval was erected, partly as a chapel for the Inca prince. In its rear was the sacred field of maize which used to be reaped by the young knights after the feast of the Huarachicu. Here Paullu lived and died, watching the total destruction of his country and people. Here his sons, Don Carlos Inca and Don Felipe Inca, were born and brought up, Carlos living quietly with his Spanish wife, and looked up to as their chief by the numerous Inca kindred in their different ayllus. Thus one son of the great Inca Huayna Ccapac made terms with the invaders, and lived on sufferance in the old palace overlooking the city of Cuzco, while the other gallantly maintained his independence in the fastnesses of Vilcapampa.

Manco was surrounded by numerous relations and followers, and lived in some state. Buildings were erected to take the places of the temple of the sun and the palace of Cuzco, and all the approaches were watched and guarded. Though very mountainous, the region between the Apurimac and Vilcamayu, called Vilcapampa, is not unproductive. There are pastures and terraced ravines, while to the north there, are tropical forests inhabited by the friendly tribe of Mañaris. Vilcapampa, with a width of forty miles, is a knot of mountains between the rivers Apurimac on the west and Vilcamayu on the east side, and with a bend of the latter river also bounding it to the north. Pizarro tried to come to terms with the Inca, but Manco had a profound distrust of Spanish promises. He therefore refused to negotiate, and Pizarro, in revenge, having taken one of Manco's wives prisoner with other Indians, stripped and flogged her, and then shot her to death with arrows. This forced Manco to make reprisals on Spaniards surprised on the roads leading to Cuzco.

After the final defeat of young Almagro by the Governor Cristoval Vaca de Castro, the lad himself and ten of his followers were executed, and many others were imprisoned at Cuzco. Two of the latter, named Gomez Perez and Diego Mendez, with six followers, escaped and took refuge in Vilcapampa. They were hospitably received by the Inca Manco, and treated with the greatest kindness. The Inca was well informed respecting passing events. When he heard that a Viceroy had arrived, named Blasco Nuñez de Vela, with orders to stop the cruelties and robberies of the Spaniards, he resolved to send an embassy offering to assist him. He selected Gomez Perez for this duty, who went to Lima, and returned with a most cordial acceptance of the Inca's offer. But the unfortunate Viceroy was driven out and finally killed by the conquerors under Gonzalo Pizarro very soon afterwards.

This Gomez Perez was a rough, ill-conditioned ruffian with a violent temper. One day he was playing at bowls with the Inca, and became so intolerably insolent that Manco pushed him, saying: 'Begone, and remember to whom you are speaking.' Perez, in a violent passion, seized the wooden ball and gave the Inca such a violent blow that he fell dead. The Indians rushed on the Spaniards, who took refuge in their lodging, defending the entrance with their swords. The Indians then set the house on fire, and all the eight ruffians were shot down with arrows as they ran out from the flames.

The Inca Manco was a worthy representative of his great ancestors. Subjected to a mock coronation and a mock sovereignty by the invaders, as soon as he reached an age of maturity he scorned such a life. Escaping from his jailers, he collected an army to strike a blow for freedom. He led his countrymen, who were devoted to him, with the utmost gallantry and some skill. He desisted from the hopeless struggle mainly to stop further bloodshed among his people. But he maintained his independence in Vilcapampa, watching events. He died, full of hope from the new Viceroy and the new laws, after a reign of ten years.

Inca Manco left three sons, named Sayri Tupac, Titu Cusi Yupanqui, and Tupac Amaru, and a daughter named Maria Tupac Usca, married to Don Pedro Ortiz de Orue, who was Encomendero of the village of Maras, with a house in Cuzco.

Sayri Tupac succeeded his father, but, as he was not yet of age, regents or tutors conducted the government of Vilcapampa.

CHAPTER XVII. GARCILASSO INCA DE LA VEGA

THE Spanish conquerors were captivated by the charms of Inca princesses and their attendants at Cuzco. Three daughters of Huayna Ccapac had Spanish husbands. Beatriz Ñusta married Mancio Serra de Leguisamo, one of the conquerors, to whom much interest attaches owing to his remarkable will. Another, Beatriz Ñusta, was the wife of Martin de Mustincia, and secondly of Diego Hernandez. Inez Ñusta had two children by Francisco Pizarro. A niece of Huayna Ccapac, named Francisca Ñusta, married Juan de Collantes, and was ancestress of Bishop Piedrahita the historian. Angelina, daughter of Atahualpa, married Juan de Betanzos, the author and Quichua scholar.

Hualpa Tupac Yupanqui, the next brother of the Inca Huayna Ccapac, had a son of the same names, and a daughter named Isabel Yupanqui Ñusta, the wife of the Spanish knight, Garcilasso de la Vega, and mother of the famous Inca historian. Paullu Tupac Yupanqui, the brother of the Inca Manco, had thrown in his lot with the Spaniards, was baptised with the name of Cristoval in 1543, and received a grant of the Colcampata palace, overlooking Cuzco. He married Catalina Mama Usica, his cousin, and had two sons, Carlos and Felipe. Prince Paullu died in May 1549.

Garcilasso de la Vega, third son of Don Alonzo de Hinestrosa de Vargas and of Doña Blanca Sotomayor Suarez de Figueroa, was born at Badajos, and was a knight of very noble lineage. His great pride was in his descent from that famous warrior, Garci Perez de Vargas, who fought by the side of St. Ferdinand at the taking of Seville in 1348. Another ancestor was Garcilasso, who received the name of de la Vega in memory of a famous duel fought with a gigantic Moor in the Vega of Granada.

> Garcilasso de la Vega,
> They the youth thenceforward call,
> For his duel in the Vega
> Of Granada chanced to fall.

Another ancestor was Diego de Mendoza, who saved the life of King Juan I at the battle of Aljubarrota. The Duke of Feria was the head of his mother's family, and he was also related to the Mendozas, Dukes of Infantado.

Born in 1506, young Garcilasso de la Vega was well practised in the use of arms when, in 1531, at the age of twenty-five, he set out for the New World as a captain of infantry with Alonzo de Alvarado, who was returning to resume his government of Guatemala. On hearing of the riches of Peru, Alvarado sailed with a large fleet from Nicaragua, and landed in the bay of Carangues in May 1534. Garcilasso de la Vega was with him, and shared all the terrible hardships and sufferings of the subsequent march to Riobamba. After the convention with Almagro, and the dispersal of Alvarado's forces, Garcilasso was sent to complete the conquest of the country round Buenaventura. He and his small band of followers forced their way through dense forests, enduring almost incredible hardships. He next went to Lima, and marched thence for the relief of Cuzco, which was surrounded by a native army under the Inca Manco. He returned to Lima after the siege, and was an officer under another Alvarado, when he was sent by Pizarro to dislodge Almagro from Cuzco. Defeated in the battle of Abancay, Garcilasso suffered a long imprisonment until the final overthrow of Almagro in April 1538. Afterwards he accompanied Gonzalo Pizarro in his conquest of Charcas, and received a grant of land near Cochabamba. He then became a citizen of Cuzco, and married the Princess Isabel Yupanqui Ñusta, formerly called Chimpa Ocllo. A contemporary portrait depicts a delicate-looking girl with large, gentle eyes and slightly aquiline nose, long black tresses hanging over her shoulders, and a richly ornamented woollen mantle secured in front by a large golden pin. Their house was at the north-west angle of the Cusi-pata, or that part of the great square which was on the west side of the Huatanay torrent. It was next door to the house of the Princess Beatriz, married to Mancio Serra de Leguisamo. From that time, though he was often away for long periods during the civil wars, the events of the life of the elder Garcilasso were closely entwined with those of his young son, the Inca.

The son of the knight Garcilasso de la Vega by the Inca princess was born in their house at Cuzco on the 12th of April 1539. His earliest recollection was of the beautiful view from the balcony. He looked down into the *catu* or market, and on his right was the convent of La Merced, where the Almagros and Gonzalo Pizarro were buried. The house had a long balcony over the entrance, where the principal lords of the city assembled to witness the bull fights and cane tournaments, which took place in the square. There was a view of the splendid snowy peak of Vilcañota, 'like a pyramid, and so lofty that, though twenty-five leagues away, and though other mountains intervene, it could be seen from the balcony. It does not appear as a mass of rock, but as a peak of pure and perpetual snow without ever melting. Its name means a sacred and wonderful thing.'

The young Inca's grown-up male relations at Cuzco were his father's brother, Juan Vargas, his father's cousin, Garcia Sanchez de Figueroa, and the brother of his mother, Hualpa Tupac Yupanqui, besides Prince Paullu and the husbands of his cousins the princesses, Mancio Serra de Leguisamo, Juan de Betanzos and Diego Hernandez. There were children of these and other native women, called mestizos, or half-castes, with whom the young Inca Garcilasso associated, and who were his friends and schoolfellows. A year before the boy's birth his father was away fighting on the side of Vaca de Castro at the battle of Chupas, where he was severely wounded. His absences were so long and frequent, that he had a friend named Diego de Alcobasa to live in the house and look after his interests. The young Inca called him his 'Ayo,' or tutor, and the two young Alcobasas were brought up almost as brothers. Young Garcilasso's godfather was Diego de Silva, a citizen and alcalde.

The education question was a very difficult one for the young mestizos during all the turmoil of civil wars, with the long paternal absences. At first they got a priest named Pedro Sanchez, and when he deserted them they were taught and disciplined by a worthy canon of the cathedral named Juan de Cuellar, a native of Medina del Campo. He read Latin with them for two years amidst the clash of arms, amidst rumours of wars and actual fighting, having undertaken the task out of kindness, and at the request of the boys themselves. The school numbered eighteen:

1. Garcilasso Inca de la Vega
2. Carlos Inca
3. Felipe Inca
4. Francisco Pizarro
5. Juan Serra de Leguisamo
6. Diego de Alcobasa
7. Francisco de Alcobasa
8. Juan de Cillorico
9. Bartolomé Monedero
10. Juan Arias Maldonado
11. Gaspar Centeno
12. Pedro Altamirano
13. Francisco Altamirano
14. A son of Garcia Sanchez de Figueroa
15. A son of Pedro de Candia
16. }
17. } Sons of Pedro del Barco
18. }

They were all eager to learn, Felipe Inca being the most clever. But the good canon was pleased with them all, seeing how much aptitude they displayed for grammar and the sciences. He used to say, 'O sons! what a pity it is that a dozen of you should not be in the university of Salamanca.'

Out of school hours they amused themselves in the best way they could. Atahualpa was naturally hated by the Incas of Cuzco, and to insult his memory the boys used to make the night hideous by using his name to imitate the crowing of a cock. The Inca describes the music as

2 crochets, 1 minim, 1 semibreve, 4 notes all on one key.

They treated his generals who had four syllables in their names in the same way—Chalcuchima, Rumi-ñaui, and Quilliscancha. They often went up to the fortress to explore the Inca ruins, which within ten years had all been taken away to build houses in the city. They ventured into the subterranean passages, and passed much time in tobogganing down the grooves in the Rodadero rock. They also had more sensible amusements, and went out hawking with the small falcons of the country, at Quepaypa. This is the fatal spot where the Incas surrendered and made submission to the generals of Atahualpa. The greatest excitement was when new animals and new fruits arrived from Spain for the first time. The first bullocks in the plough, the property of Juan Rodriguez de Villalobos, appeared near Cuzco in 1550. The young Inca went off to see them, with a great crowd, when he ought to have been at school. The land ploughed was just above the convent of St. Francis, and the names of the bullocks were *Chaparro, Naranjo,* and *Castillo*. It was a marvellous sight for the boy, but he had to pay for acting truant. His father flogged him, and the schoolmaster gave him another flogging because his father had not given him enough. The next wonder was a donkey which his father had bought at Guamanga to breed mules from his mares.

Horses were very precious and very dear. But this did not restrain the young mestizos from riding races down the streets of Cuzco. Antonio de Altamirano, father of the Altamirano boys, was very rich. He had received one half of the palace of Huayna Ccapac, and found hidden there an immense haul of gold and silver cups and vases. He could afford to keep several horses, and his sons could mount their schoolfellows. One day they were riding a race, and a very pretty girl watched them from a window. Pedro Altamirano kept looking back at her, until at last he fell off. But the horse stopped for him to mount again. Their father was the first person in Cuzco who owned cows. Unfortunately both the Altamirano boys died young, 'to the great grief of the whole city, by reason of the promise they gave of ability and virtue.'

Wonders continued to present themselves to the astonished eyes of young Garcilasso. A knight named Bartolomé de Terraças was the first to send grapes to Cuzco. The bunches were sent to the elder Garcilasso to distribute among the citizens. His son had to take the dishes to each house, attended by two young Indian pages, and of course he did not fail to enjoy a good share himself by the way. He was not so fortunate with the asparagus. The Treasurer Garcia de Melo could only send three stalks to his father, who cooked them at the *brasero* in his own room, sent his son for salt and pepper, and gave a tiny bit to each of his guests. But young Garcilasso got none, although he had brought the trimmings.

The young Inca's mother and her family were well acquainted with the virtues of many herbs and roots. There was one very formidable white root, which was pounded, put in water, and given to young Garcilasso to drink when he had a stomach-ache. It was a drastic remedy. First it made him feel sick, and in half an hour he was so giddy that he could not stand. Then he felt as if ants were crawling over his body and down his veins. He next felt as if he was going to die. When the medicine had finished working he was left quite well, with a tremendous appetite. He himself effected a signal cure on a boy named Martin, son of Pedro Fernandez the loyal, who was suffering from a sore and inflamed eye. Garcilasso took a plant called *matecllu*, which is found in streams, a foot long with one round leaf at the end. He mashed it, and applied it as a poultice to his friend, who was cured after two applications. Afterwards he saw Martin in Spain in 1611, when he was head groom to the Duke of Feria, and he said that he saw better in that eye than in the other.

As Garcilasso grew up he exchanged his boyish games and excursions for the more serious cane tournaments, requiring much practice. He played in the tournaments on the feast of Santiago five times, also at the baptism of Inca Sayri Tupac, when he rode a young horse which had not completed its third year.

The youth Garcilasso was a born topographer, with a remarkable memory. Forty years after he left Cuzco he described the city, with the exact positions of the houses of sixty-six Spanish citizens. Little had been altered in his youth. He remembered three of the great covered halls attached to the palaces of the Incas, 200 paces long by 50, one in the Amaru-cancha or palace of Huayna Ccapac, now the church of the Jesuits, another in the Cassana or palace of Pachacuti, capable of holding 4000 people, and another on the Colcampata. The great hall of the palace of Uira-cocha, on the east side of the great square, was in process of being converted into the cathedral.

The first great trouble remembered by the young Inca was when Gonzalo Pizarro rose against the Viceroy Blasco Nuñez de Vela and the new laws. The Cuzco citizens were forced to join if they did not escape. The elder Garcilasso de la Vega, Pedro del Barco, Antonio Altamirano, and Hernando Bachicao fled to Lima. The three last, two of them fathers of the young Inca's schoolfellows, were hanged by Pizarro's cruel old lieutenant Carbajal. Garcilasso was concealed for weeks in the convent of San Francisco at Lima, but at last Gonzalo Pizarro pardoned him. He was kept as a sort of prisoner, and obliged to accompany the rebels. Meanwhile the house at Cuzco was attacked by the Pizarro faction, and besieged. The garrison consisted of the young Inca with his mother and sister, the Alcobasas, and two faithful maids. They were nearly starved, and when the besiegers got in, the house was pillaged. At last Diego Centeno arrived with the Inca's uncle, Juan Vargas, and the family was relieved. They had been living on alms.

Centeno advanced to Lake Titicaca, where the battle of Huarina was fought on October 25, 1547. Gonzalo Pizarro was victorious, and marched triumphantly to Cuzco. Centeno fled, and Juan Vargas was killed, to the great grief of his brother and nephew. Garcilasso de la Vega was forced to accompany the rebels, and was an unwilling spectator of the battle of Huarina, where his brother lost his life on the loyal side. He had to lend his favourite horse 'Salinillas' to Gonzalo Pizarro, and to go with him in his triumphant march northwards.

On the approach of the rebels, the little Inca went out of Cuzco to meet his father, as far as Quispicancha, over ten miles. He went partly on foot and partly on the backs of two Indian servants. The meeting must have been a very joyful one, for the family had suffered much during the father's absence. They gave the little boy a horse for the return journey. Gonzalo Pizarro entered Cuzco triumphantly, with such bells as there were ringing joyful peals. There was an interval of nearly five months and a half between his victory at Huarina and his defeat and death at Sacsahuana. Young Garcilasso says that the great rebel treated him as if he had been his own son. The Inca was much in Gonzalo's house, and, though barely nine years old, he dined twice at the Procurator's table in company with his cousin and schoolfellow Francisco Pizarro, the son of the Marquis. Gonzalo Pizarro amused himself by making the two boys have running and jumping matches, until a rivalry was created between the young competitors.

Then came the rout of Sacsahuana on April 8, 1548, when the elder Garcilasso took the opportunity of galloping over to the royalist side on his favourite horse 'Salinillas,' which had been returned to him by Gonzalo. The interment of the headless body of Gonzalo Pizarro in the church of La Merced quickly followed. Then there were some years of peace, and young Garcilasso eagerly gathered knowledge as his age increased. He listened, with the deepest interest, when his mother's relations came to their house and conversed on the majesty and grandeur of the Incas, their government and laws. Soon he began to ask questions, and was told of the mythical origin of his ancestors, of the settling of the city, and the deeds of Manco Ccapac. On other occasions he listened to the conversations of the Spanish conquerors, when they fought their battles over again with his father. He also had opportunities of examining the *quipus* of his father's vassals when they came to pay their tribute at Christmas or St. John's. Comparing the tribute with the knots, he soon came to understand their system of accounts by *quipus*.

Another civil war was impending. The President of the Audiencia, Pedro de la Gasca, so undeservedly praised by Prescott, had left the country seething with discontent, and in a most unsettled state. At last the storm burst at Cuzco, the malcontents having secretly planned a rising under the leadership of Francisco Hernandez Giron. Young Garcilasso had lost his mother a .few years before, and his father had married a Spanish lady.

On November 13, 1553, there was a marriage at Cuzco of Don Alonso de Loaysa, nephew of the Archbishop of Lima, with a young lady named Maria de Castilla, and a grand wedding supper was given in the evening. The ladies supped separately in an inner room. Young Garcilasso came rather late, to return with his father and step-mother. The Corregidor was presiding, and the lad was just sitting down at his invitation, when the street door was thrown violently open, and Giron stalked in with his drawn sword, followed by two men armed with partisans. The company started to their feet, two were killed and then the lights were put out. The Corregidor ran into the room of the ladies, who were not molested, but he was taken prisoner. The Garcilassos, father and son, with some others, found a passage which led into the back-yard. They all climbed up on to the roof of the house next door, which belonged to Juan de Figueroa. Thence they got into a back street. Young Garcilasso was sent forward as a scout until they reached the house of his father's brother-in-law, Antonio de Quiñones. They had married sisters. It took a little time for young Garcilasso to get horses ready, but before midnight his father and Quiñones had galloped out of Cuzco, on their way to Lima. The young Inca was left in charge of his step -mother. The Giron rebellion lasted for a year, ending with the battle of Pucara on October 24, 1554.

The elder Garcilasso became Corregidor of Cuzco in 1555, and his son began to be very useful to him. The father's estates were at Tapacri, near Cochabamba, at Cotonera, Huamanpalpa, and the coca plantation of Abisca. The son visited these properties, and also acted as his father's secretary during his term of office. Both were very busy collecting subscriptions for the erection of a hospital for Indians, of which the elder Garcilasso laid the first stone. The good knight showed great kindness to the young sons of Pedro del Barco, who were left fatherless and destitute.

The Viceroy, Don Andres Hurtado de Mendoza, Marquis of Cañete, arrived at Lima in July 1555. He was very anxious that the young Inca Sayri Tupac should consent to come out of Vilcapampa, and live with the Spaniards. He wrote to the Corregidor of Cuzco and to the Princess Beatriz, wife of Leguisamo, asking them to make the necessary arrangements. It was a difficult matter, requiring skilful diplomacy, for the Inca's tutors were fearful of treachery. Juan Betanzos was sent, but was not allowed to enter the Inca's territory. Only the princess's son, Juan Serra de Leguisamo, was permitted to reach the presence of the Inca with the Viceroy's rich presents. After much deliberation Sayri Tupac consented to go to Lima, carried in a litter. He was very cordially received by the Viceroy and Archbishop, and granted a pension and an estate in the valley of Vilcamayu. Sayri Tupac then began the journey to Cuzco. At Guamanga he was presented, by a knight named Miguel Astete, with the *llautu*, or fringe of sovereignty, which had been taken from Atahualpa.

Sayri Tupac lived in the house of his aunt, the Princess Beatriz, while he was at Cuzco, and all those of the blood-royal went there to kiss his hand. Among others, the young Inca Garcilasso waited upon his cousin, and they drank chicha together out of silver cups. The Inca Sayri Tupac was married to Cusi Huarcay, a granddaughter of the ill-fated Inca Huascar. They were both baptised at Cuzco, and then proceeded to the abode assigned to them near Yucay. Sayri Tupac died in 1560. His daughter, Clara Beatriz, married Don Martin Garcia Loyola, a nephew of St. Ignatius. Their daughter Lorenza was created Marquesa de Oropesa in her own right, with remainder to the descendants of her great-uncle, Tupac Amaru. She married Juan Henriquez de Borja, a grandson of the Duke of Gandia.

The last year of the abode of the young Inca Garcilasso in the home of his childhood was a very melancholy one. His father was suffering from a long and painful illness. He died in 1559, and his son, now in his twentieth year, was left alone in the world. It was settled that he should realise what worldly possessions he could get together, and seek his fortune in the mother country. When he went to take leave of the Corregidor, Polo de Ondegardo, that body-snatching official showed him the mummies of three Incas and two Ccoyas, which he had found after a prolonged search. He called them Uira-cocha, Tupac Yupanqui, Huayna Ccapac, Mama Runtu and Mama Ocllo. The Incas were in their ceremonial dresses, and wore the *llautu*.

On January 23, 1560, the Inca Garcilasso left Cuzco never to return. There are a few glimpses of the young exile during his journey. His first halt was at Marca Huasi, nine leagues from Cuzco, an estate owned by Pedro Lopez de Cacalla, secretary to La Gasca. The manager took him over the vineyards, but did not offer him any grapes, for which he was longing. The excuse was that they were grown to make wine, to compete for a prize. Garcilasso next turns up in the valley of Huarcu, or Cañete, on the coast, where he hears of the wonderful harvests of wheat. On the voyage he was becalmed for three days off Cape Pasaos, in 0 20 S. He mentions being at Panama and Carthagena, and in 1562 he was at Madrid, where he saw Hernando Pizarro and Las Casas. The good Bishop gave the young mestizo his hand to kiss, but when he found that the youth was from Peru, and not from Mexico, he had little to say to him.

Garcilasso de la Vega does not appear to have been welcomed with any very great amount of cordiality by his grand relations in Spain. How he must have regretted his happy boyhood at Cuzco, and the loss of all his friends! At first he got some letters from his cousin Figueroa, and his Inca uncle, Hualpa Tupac Yupanqui.

The young Inca made an application for the restitution of the patrimony of his mother, and for a recognition of his father's faithful services. It was referred to the Council of the Indies, and the members were convinced by his proofs until an ill-natured lawyer named Lope Garcia de Castro intervened. He was afterwards Governor of Peru from 1564 to 1569. He asked the Inca what favour he could expect when his father was at the battle of Huarina helping Gonzalo Pizarro. Garcilasso replied that it was false. Castro then said that three historians had affirmed it, and who was he to deny what they said? So his petition was rejected. His best friend at this sad time, and for long afterwards, was Don Alonzo Fernandez de Cordova, Lord of the House of Aguilar, and Marquis of Priego, a Figueroa cousin of Garcilasso on his grandmother's side.

The Inca obtained a captaincy in the army of Philip II, and served in the campaign against the Moriscos under Don Juan of Austria. He soon afterwards left a military life, poor and in debt, and devoted himself to literary pursuits. His first production was a translation from the Italian of the 'Dialogues of Love' by a Jew named Abarbanel, who wrote under the *nom de plume of El Leon Ebreo*. The Inca's translation was published in 1590. The dedication to the King contains a full account of Garcilasso's Inca lineage.

His next work was a narrative of the expedition of Hernando de Soto in Florida, which he completed in 1591. He is said to have got his information chiefly from the accounts of an old soldier who served with de Soto. It was first published at Lisbon in 1605, and reprinted several times. The best edition is that of 1722.

Don Pascual de Gayangos gave me a curious manuscript written by the Inca, which appears to have been intended for a dedicatory epistle to be placed at the beginning of the Inca's work on Florida. It is addressed to the head of the Vargas family, and consists of a full genealogical account of the house of Vargas, followed by an abstract of the contents of the work on Florida, and an explanation of the system adopted by the author in its division into six books. In the genealogical part there are several interesting digressions, both personal and historical.

We gather from this document that his uncle, Don Alonzo de Vargas, a military officer of long and varied service, being childless, adopted the Inca as his heir.

For many years before his death Garcilasso had lived in a hired house in the city of Cordova—'mi pobre casa de alquiler.' He was never married. As years rolled on he began to think more of the land of his birth, and, as we can gather from the above document, he had resolved to write the story of his native land in 1596, the date of the document.

In that or the next year a Jesuit residing at Cordova, named Maldonado de Saavedra, a native of Seville, gave the Inca the history of Peru by Blas Valera, a manuscript written in most elegant Latin. The Inca says that only one half was rescued from pillage during the sack of Cadiz by the English. But the priests were allowed to take their papers with them, and Dr. Gonzalez de la Rosa thinks that Garcilasso received the history intact. He speaks with great respect of the knowledge and learning of Blas Valera, quoting twenty-one passages from his work, most of them long and important. For a narrative of the events of each Inca's reign, Garcilasso wrote to his old schoolfellows asking them to help him by sending him accounts of conquests of the Incas in the countries of their mothers, for each province has its *quipus* and recorded annals and traditions. He adds that they sent them to him, and that he thus got the records of the deeds of the Incas. His great friend Diego de Alcobasa had become a priest, and he sent a valuable account of the ruins of Tiahuanacu. But Garcilasso mentions no others by name. The cruel edict of Toledo had banished and scattered his mestizo schoolfellows. It is difficult to avoid a suspicion that the narratives of historical events are based on the history of Blas Valera and unacknowledged, and not on communications from his schoolfellows. Garcilasso further says that his plan is to relate what he heard in his childhood from his mother and her relations respecting the origin of the Incas.

His work is divided into two parts, the first containing a history of the Incas and their civilisation, and the second being a record of the Spanish conquest and subsequent civil wars. The title is, 'The Royal Commentaries of Peru.' The first part received the approval and licence of the Inquisition in 1604, and was published at Lisbon in 1609, dedicated to the Duchess of Braganza. The second part appeared at Cordova in 1617, after the author's death, 'by the widow of Andres Barrera and at her cost.'

The work is, in fact, a commentary to a large extent. For events, and accounts of religious rites and customs, he quotes largely from other authors, sometimes adding criticisms of their statements. The authors he quotes are: Blas Valera, twenty-one times; Cieza de Leon, thirty times; Acosta, twenty-seven times; Gomara, eleven times; Zarate, nine times; Fernandez twice; and his friends Alcobasa and Figueroa seven times. His own personal reminiscences are by far the most interesting passages, and they are scattered about everywhere throughout both parts.

The 'Royal Commentaries' were, until quite recently, the most valued authority for Peruvian civilisation and the history of the Incas. The position of the writer as an Inca on the mother's side, the fulness of detail both as regards the history and the manners, customs, and religion of the people, and the peculiar charm of his style fully account for the position his work held for so long. Prescott quotes Garcilasso twice as often as any other authority. But the Inca was writing forty years after he had left the country. Sarmiento now, to a great extent, supersedes his history. Molina, Morua, Blas Valera, Salcamayhua, and other writers whose works have recently come to light, are more reliable as regards the religion and manners and customs of the people, because they wrote on the spot and with fuller knowledge. Dr. Gonzalez de la Rosa has shown reason for questioning Garcilasso's integrity as regards the use of the manuscript of Blas Valera. Yet, in spite of all this, the Inca will continue to be an important authority, while the charm of his personal reminiscences must ever have a fascination for his readers from which no criticism can detract.

The Inca must have led a somewhat lonely bachelor's life at Cordova, yet it can scarcely have been an unhappy one, when his occupation filled him constantly with happy remembrances of his boyhood. He had the pleasure of welcoming at least one of his schoolfellows. This was Juan Arias Maldonado, son of Maldonado the rich. He had been robbed of his estates and driven out of the country by the cruel tyrant Toledo. He had obtained leave to return to Peru for three years, to recover some of his property. Before sailing he came to the Inca at Cordova with his wife. They were in great poverty, and the Inca gave them all the white clothing he possessed, and much cloth and taffeta. They reached the bay of Payta, where Juan Arias died of joy at once more seeing his native land.

In 1603 the Inca was deeply interested in the efforts of his mother's family to obtain some small modicum of justice. Melchior Carlos Inca, the son of his unfortunate old schoolfellow Carlos Inca, accompanied by Don Alonso de Mesa, son of one of the best of the conquerors, had come to Spain to petition for his rights. The few surviving Incas wrote to empower Garcilasso, Alonso de Mesa, and Melchior to act for them in striving to obtain immunity for them from many vexatious and ruinous imposts. They also sent proofs of their descent painted on a yard and a half of white silk of China, with the Incas in their ancient dresses. The covering letter was dated April 16, 1603, and signed by four Incas, each one representing an *ayllu*. There were then 567 agnates of the royal family. In 1604 Melchior Carlos Inca received a grant of 7500 ducats a year in perpetuity from the Lima treasury, and was invested with the order of Santiago. He was not allowed to return to Peru, and he died at Alcala de Henares in 1610. His only son died in the same year, and thus the main line of Prince Paullu became extinct. Nothing could be effected for the Inca petitioners. Most of them, with many of their mestizo relations, perished in misery and exile.

Garcilasso Inca de la Vega was a devoted son of the Church. In his last years he was much occupied in the preparation of a side-chapel in the cathedral of Cordova for his interment. It was to be dedicated to the souls in purgatory. From his will we gather that his house was fairly well furnished, that he had a gold jewel inlaid with a diamond, and a grandfather's clock. His plate for table and sideboard was sufficient for his rank, and his accoutrements during the Morisco war were hanging on his walls: a cutlass, a battle-axe, an engraved helmet, a halberd, and spurs. A cage with five canary birds hung by the old man's chair. There were two bookcases and a stand for papers. On September 18, 1612, he had bought the chapel in the cathedral from the Bishop, and he left a number of other legal documents, including the will of his uncle and guardian, Alonzo de Vargas, dated 1570. The Inca was well supplied with linen sheets and pillow-cases for his beds, as well as mattresses and counterpanes.

The old Inca's household consisted of Diego de Vargas, whom he had brought up, Beatriz de Vega, a captive slave named Marina de Cordova, Maria de Prados, an orphan child brought up by him, and a lad named Francisco. By his will he emancipated Marina, and left them all small pensions, their beds and chests, and all the wheat, bacon, and wine in the house, to be divided equally.

Masses were to be said daily in his mortuary chapel, a lamp was to be kept burning in it, and there was to be a salary for the sacristan. Funds were provided of which the Dean and Chapter were appointed trustees.

The Inca Garcilasso de la Vega died in his house in the parish of Santa Maria in Cordova on April 22, 1616, just ten days after his seventy-seventh birthday. He was buried in the chapel he had purchased and restored, in the cathedral of Cordova. Visitors are fascinated by the wonderful beauty of the interior, with its forests of pillars, with its memories of the Beni Umeyyah, and the exquisite Mihrab of Hakem II. Perhaps a few may find time to give a thought to the good old Inca. His chapel is on the north side, the third from the east. His arms are over the iron grating and gate. On the dexter side are Vargas quartering Figueroa, Saavedra, and Mendoza, and impaling the arms granted to the Incas. These are azure two serpents supporting a rainbow from their mouths, from which hangs the *llautu*, in chief a sun and moon. The stone covering the tomb is in the centre of the little chapel. The epitaph painted on boards is on each side of the altar. On the gospel side:

'The Inca Garcilasso de la Vega, a distinguished man worthy of perpetual memory, illustrious in blood, well versed in letters, valiant in arms. Son of Garcilasso de la Vega of the ducal houses of Feria and Infantado, and of

Elizabeth Palla, sister of Huaina Ccapac, last Emperor of Peru. He edited La Florida, translated Leon Ebreo, composed the Royal Commentaries.'

On the epistle side:

'He lived very religiously in Cordova, died, and was buried in this chapel. He closed up his estate in a chain for the good of souls in purgatory, being perpetual trustees the Dean and Chapter of this holy church. He died on the 22nd of April, 1616.'

'Pray to God for his soul.'

A lamp hangs from the roof, and is always kept burning, night and day, in accordance with the clause in the Inca's will.

CHAPTER XVIII. THE LAST OF THE INCAS

THE terrible doom of the unfortunate Peruvians and their beloved Incas was now inevitable. It came upon them in one crushing blow a very little more than ten years after the departure of the Inca Garcilasso de la Vega for Europe. On the death of Sayri Tupac, his brother Titu Cusi Yupanqui was acclaimed as sovereign Inca in Vilcapampa—a man of very different mould. Juan de Betanzos and Rodriguez were sent to persuade him to follow his elder brother's example, but without effect. He was firm in the resolve to maintain his independence.

The Inca Garcilasso's old schoolfellow, Carlos Inca, had succeeded his father, Prince Paullu, at the palace of the Colcampata, and was married to a Spanish lady born in Peru, named Maria de Esquivel. Little of the palace now remains, but it is a very interesting spot and closely connected with the last days of the Incas.

High above the city, of which there is an extensive view bounded by the snowy peak of Vilcañota, and at the foot of the precipitous ascent to the fortress, is the small open space before the little church of San Cristoval. On the north side was the palace. On a terrace with a stone revetment, one may still see a wall built of stones of various sizes fitting exactly one into the other. It is seventy-four yards long and sixteen feet high. In this wall there are eight recesses at equal distances, resembling doorways. They are too shallow to be used for shelter—only two and a half inches. They could not have been used as doors, for this wall is a revetment. One only is a doorway. They are not likely to have been merely ornamental. I think that these recesses contained sacred or royal emblems of some kind. The point is interesting, as there are exactly the same walls at the palaces of Chinchero, Limatambo, and Yucay.

The third recess from the west is a doorway leading to a steep narrow staircase. Above there is a platform, now a maize-field, on a level with the top of the recessed wall, once a garden leading to and fronting the palace itself. The remains of the palace are now of very small extent. They consist of a wall of admirably worked masonry forty feet long and ten and a half feet high. The stones are beautifully cut in perfect parallelograms, all of the same height but varying in length, fitting exactly one to the other. The wall contains a doorway and a window. The sides of the doorway support a stone lintel nearly eight feet long, while a stone of similar length forms the doorstep. The window is nearly 6 ft. from the ground, 2 ft. 3 in. broad, by 2 ft. 8 in. high. The foundations and parts of the wall continue for 65 ft.; and behind there are three terraces planted with fruit trees, up to the base of the steep ascent, on the summit of which the citadel once stood.

The palace was the work of the great Inca Pachacuti at the time when he was remodelling the whole city. In imagination we can rebuild the palace from these ruins, with its approach through the revetment wall, its beautiful gardens and terraces, its long façade of exactly fitting masonry, and its great hall, which we are told by Garcilasso was intact in his time. Pachacuti called it the *Llactapata*, and desired to be interred there. The more modern term Colcampata may have been given owing to granaries (colca) having been placed there at some later time.

Here dwelt Carlos Inca with his wife Maria de Esquivel, as the head of the section of his family that had submitted to the Spaniards. His relations, driven from their homes in the city, lived in the suburbs and the neighbouring villages. The Inca received frequent visits from them, and appears to have held a somewhat melancholy court. Carlos was the depositary of a great secret. Between the time when the transmission of Atahualpa's ransom was stopped, owing to his murder, and the arrival of Pizarro at Cuzco, the respite was employed in secretly concealing the vast treasure still remaining in Cuzco and the neighbourhood, which amounted to millions. It included the great golden statue which was the *Huauqui* of the Inca Huayna Ccapac, and of course was never found. It was very fortunate for Carlos Inca that the Spaniards did not know of the secret, or that he was its depositary. It is said that once, when his wife taunted him with his poverty, Carlos led her, under promise of secrecy, blindfold to the secret place, and took her breath away at the sight of such vast treasure. He handed the secret down to a successor when he went into exile.

It is now time to introduce the villain of the piece. Don Francisco de Toledo was a younger son of the Count of Oropesa, belonging to a family of which the butcher Alva was the head. Don Francisco was advanced in years when he came to Peru as Viceroy in 1569, and resolved to visit every part of the vast territory under his rule. He was accompanied by Agustin de la Coruña, Bishop of Popayan, the author Josef de Acosta, the lawyers Polo de Ondegardo and Juan de Matienza, the cosmographer Pedro Sarmiento, the secretary Navamuel, and some others. Toledo was an indefatigable worker, but excessively narrow-minded, cruel and pitiless. One of his ideas was to prove that the King of Spain had a right to Peru because the Incas were usurpers. With this object he examined a number of leading Indians at every place he stopped at, but they were not *Amautas* versed in history, and their evidence is of little or no value. He sent it all to Spain in reports, which have recently been published. This Viceroy arrived at Cuzco early in the year 1571. There were bull fights, tournaments, and other displays in his honour.

At nearly the same time the wife of Don Carlos Inca gave birth to a son and heir, and the Viceroy was requested to be godfather to the child, and 'compadre' or gossip to its parents. He consented, and the baptismal ceremony took place in the little church of San Cristoval. This edifice is built of ancient masonry, and must once have been part of the palace. The child received the names of Carlos Melchior. All the *ayllus* of the Incas were present, and when the company adjourned to the palace there were rejoicings, dances, fireworks, and 'many newly invented and costly conceits.' The Viceroy came up the staircase in the revetment wall into the gardens of the palace, like a bird of evil omen, guarded by halberdiers. He is portrayed as a short dark man of fifty, with narrow forehead, hawk's nose, black eyes, and a saturnine expression. He would have been in a black velvet suit, with the green cross of Alcantara embroidered on his doublet—certainly a wet blanket.

It is alleged that the Inca Titu Cusi Yupanqui, with his young brother Tupac Amaru, was present and mingled among the crowd of guests. He was impressed with the ceremony, and soon afterwards sent envoys to Cuzco to request that persons might be sent to him to instruct him in the Christian religion. Two friars named Juan de Vivero, who had baptised Sayri Tupac and was Prior of the Augustine convent, and Diego Ortiz, also one of the Augustine order, were despatched with three laymen as companions, and a mestizo servant named Pando. Diego Rodriguez de Figueroa also came as Chief Magistrate and leader of the party, which entered the fastnesses of Vilcapampa and was well received. Rodriguez wrote an account of the mission, which has been preserved. He describes how, when courtiers entered to the presence of Titu Cusi, they first did *mucha* or reverence to the sun and then to the Inca. The Spaniards used all the arts of persuasion they possessed to induce Titu Cusi to follow the example of his brother and surrender to the conquerors. This he would not do. He temporised and procrastinated for so long that the embassy returned. Friar Ortiz and Pando remained behind. The Inca had been baptised by Father Vivero, receiving the name of Felipe.

Then the Inca had a mortal illness. Pando, the interpreter, had told wonderful stories about the miraculous powers of the Christian priests, so Friar Ortiz was ordered to restore the Inca to health; and he began to say daily masses. The Inca died, and as the fault was naturally supposed to be with the priest and his interpreter, they were put to death. Meanwhile another embassy was sent before the news of the Inca's death had arrived. The chiefs were thoroughly alarmed, and when the envoy Atilano de Añaya attempted to force an entrance by the bridge of Chuqui-chaca he also was put to death.

The deceased Inca was jealous of his younger brother, Tupac Amaru, and confined him in the House of the Sun, in accordance with an ancient usage, keeping him secluded, on the ground of his inexperience.

Tupac Amaru, who, judging from the date of his father's death must have been at least twenty-five years of age, was already married and had two daughters and a little son. After the deaths of Ortiz, Pando, and Añaya, the chiefs brought Tupac Amaru out of his seclusion, so that he was not responsible for these deaths, and was indeed perfectly innocent. He was acclaimed as Sovereign Inca. The *llautu*, or fringe, was placed on his head, the *yacolla*, or mantle, was fastened over his shoulders, the *chipana*, or bracelet, was clasped round his wrist. Then the *achihua*, or parasol, was held over him while he was invested with the *tumi*, or knife, *chuqui*, or lance, *huallcanca*, or shield, and *usuta*, or shoes. Finally he was carried in the *huantuy*, or litter, to the *tiana*, or throne, and was solemnly crowned with the *mascapaycha*, or imperial head-dress, over the *llautu*.

The deaths of Ortiz and Pando furnished the Viceroy Toledo with an excuse for the invasion and conquest of Vilcapampa. He assembled as large a force as he could muster, which was placed under the command of Martin Hernando de Arbieto, a veteran of the civil wars. His captains were Juan Alvarez Maldonado, father of Garcilasso's schoolfellow; Martin Garcia de Loyola, captain of the Viceroy's bodyguard; Mancio Serra de Leguisamo, father of another of Garcilasso's schoolfellows; and nine others. They marched down the valley of Vilcamayu to the bridge of Chuqui-chaca, which is the key of Vilcapampa by the western door. Another force watched the outlets on the side of Apancay and the Apurimac. The Incas made some resistance, and then retreated to their camp under a heavy fire of arquebuses and field-pieces. Next day the Indians fled along a narrow path, with dense undergrowth on one side and a precipice on the other. The Spaniards followed, often in single file. At one place a gallant chief named Hualpa rushed out of the bushes, and grappled with Loyola, who led the vanguard. While they were struggling together, a servant named Carrillo drew Loyola's sword and killed Hualpa from behind. It was a lucky but not a chivalrous escape for the Knight of Calatrava. The pursuit was continued. The young Inca was making his way, by a valley called Simaponte, to the friendly

Mañari Indians in the montaña. They had placed canoes on a river to enable him to escape.

Loyola went in chase with fifty men and overtook the fugitives, who were captured, after a brief resistance, on October 4, 1571. When at last General Arbieto was satiated with the slaughter of unarmed Indians, he marched back to Cuzco with the Inca Tupac Amaru, his family and chiefs, as prisoners. They dressed the young sovereign in his imperial robes and headgear, put a rope round his neck, and so brought him before Toledo, a most ignoble triumph. Don Carlos Inca had been lawlessly driven out of the Colcampata in order to convert it into a prison, and here the Inca was confined. There was a mock trial, presided over by one of Toledo's creatures named Gabriel de Loarte, who condemned the Inca to be beheaded and all his chiefs to be hanged. The chiefs were tortured with such savage brutality that they died in the streets before they could reach the gallows, and the executioners had to hang the dead bodies.

The unfortunate young Inca was beset by monks in his prison, and, at the end of two days, he was baptised. On the third day he was led forth from the Colcampata, and through the streets to the great square, accompanied by four priests, one being Father Cristoval de Molina, the Quichua scholar and author. The scaffold was built in front of the cathedral. The open spaces and streets were densely crowded with sorrowing Indians. When the Inca ascended the scaffold with the priests, the executioner, a Cañari Indian, brought out the knife. 'Then,' wrote an eyewitness, 'the whole crowd of natives raised such a cry of grief that it seemed as if the day of judgment had come.' Many invoked their most venerated *huaca*, and cried out:

'AY HUANACAURI MAYTAM RICUY SAPRA AUCACHIC CHOMANA HUCHAYOCTA CONCAYQUITA INCAP CUCHON.'

'O Huanacauri! behold where the wicked and cruel enemies cut the neck of the Inca.'

Even the Spaniards were horrified, for all knew that the young man was innocent, and had committed no offence.

Things being in this state, all the chief dignitaries of the Church hurried to the Viceroy. They were the Bishop of Popayan, the Provincials of all the religious orders, and the Rector of the Jesuits. They went down on their knees and entreated the ruthless Toledo to show mercy and spare the life of the Inca. They urged that he should be sent to Spain to be judged by the King in person. But no prayers could prevail with the obstinate, pitiless man. Juan de Soto, chief officer of the court, was sent on horseback with a pole to clear the way, galloping furiously and riding down the people. He ordered the Inca's head to be cut off at once, in the name of the Viceroy.

Tupac Amaru was told that the time had come. He took one step forward and raised his right arm. Instantly there was profound silence. He then said in a loud voice:

'CCOLLANAN PACHACAMAC RICUY AUCCACUNAC YAHUARNIY HICHASCANCUTA.'
'O righteous God! behold how my enemies shed my blood.'

According to the picture by Huaman Poma, the Inca was then thrown on his back, his arms and legs were held by two men, and a third cut his throat. There was a great and bitter cry from the vast multitude. The head was cut off, and stuck on a pole. The Inca's body was carried to the house of his mother, the Queen Cusi Huarcay. All the bells in the city were tolled. Next day the body was interred in the high chapel of the cathedral, the service being performed by the chapter. Pontifical mass was said by the good Bishop of Popayan. Next day all the funeral honours were repeated, and the masses were sung with the organ.

The Inca's head remained on a pole in the great square. Mancio Serra de Leguisamo passed that night in a house to the right of the cathedral. He awoke just before dawn and thought he heard a noise such as would be caused by a vast multitude. He got up and looked out. To his utter amazement, the whole square was covered with a closely packed crowd, all kneeling, and all offering *mucha* or reverence to the Inca's head. He reported this surprising incident to the Viceroy, who promptly ordered the head to be buried with the body.

Thus ended the famous dynasty of the Incas. It formed a line of wise and capable sovereigns ruling a vast empire on such principles, and with such capacity and wisdom as the world has never seen before or since. Assuredly the story of their rise, their government, and their sorrowful end is worthy of study.

'The execrable regicide,' as Toledo is called on the Inca Pedigrees, was not yet satisfied. He had driven Carlos Inca from his property regardless of right or law. He now banished him to Lima without any suitable provision. With him were expelled his brother Felipe Inca, the clever pupil of Garcilasso's school days, and thirty-five more of the principal Incas. They all perished miserably and in poverty. Saddest of all was the fate of four poor little Inca children; neither their tender age nor their innocence saved them from Toledo's inhuman persecution. They were Quispi Titu, the son of the Inca Cusi Titu Yupanqui, little Martin, son of the murdered Inca Tupac Amaru, and his two daughters, Magdalena and Juana. The boys were received in the house of Don Martin Ampuero of Lima, son of Francisco Ampuero and his wife, who was daughter of Francisco Pizarro by the Princess Inez, daughter of Huayna Ccapac. But both the exiled boys died young.

The forlorn little girls, Magdalena and Juana Tupac Amaru, were kindly received in the house of Dr. Loaysa, the first Archbishop of Lima, who took charge of them. Juana married the Curaca of Surimani, named Condorcanqui, from whom descended the ill-fated José Gabriel Condorcanqui, who took the name of Tupac Amaru and headed a rising against the Spaniards in 1782.

The inhuman Viceroy was not even yet satisfied. He aimed at the extirpation of every branch of the royal family of Peru. He next decreed the banishment of all the mestizos, those bright and happy lads who were the schoolfellows of the Inca Garcilasso. A few, having taken orders, were overlooked. The rest were sent to perish in the swamps of Darien, or the frozen wilds of Southern Chile. This persecution of the mestizos was as stupid as it was cruel, for excellent service might have been got from them by a wise administrator.

Toledo remained for six more years in Peru, making an almost endless number of laws and ordinances, until they filled a large volume. They were worse than useless, for no attention was paid to the few just and good rules amongst them, while the wisdom and statesmanship of the majority may be judged from a few specimens taken at random:

'Any Indian who makes friendship with an Indian woman who is an infidel, is to receive one hundred lashes, for the first offence, that being the punishment they dislike most.

'Indians shall no longer use surnames taken from the moon, birds, animals, serpents, or rivers, which they formerly used.

'No Indian shall be elected for any office who has been punished for idolatry, worshipping *huacas*, dancing, mourning, or singing in memory of infidel rites, offering up chicha, coca, or burnt fat, or for dancing the dance called *Ayrihua*.'

Toledo's term of office came to an end in September 1581, a period of nearly twelve years. It was generally reported that he was received with coldness by King Philip II, who told him that he was not sent out to kill Kings but to serve Kings. Huaman Poma depicts the retired Viceroy sitting in a chair in a state of extreme despondency. This report would be very satisfactory if true. But there is some evidence that Toledo's general policy was approved, although fault may have been found with some of the details.

There can be no doubt of the disastrous results of the ruthless administration of such men as Toledo, and of the Spanish rule. The last survivor of the original conquerors has given his testimony with no uncertain sound. Mancio Serra de Leguisamo signed his will at Cuzco on September 18, 1589, with the following preamble:

'First, and before I begin my testament, I declare that for many years I have desired to take order for informing the Catholic and Royal Majesty of the King Don Felipe our Lord, seeing how Catholic and most Christian he is, and how zealous for the service of God our Lord, touching what is needed for the health of my soul, seeing that I took a great part in the discovery, conquest, and settlement of these kingdoms, when we drove out those who were the Lords Incas and who possessed and ruled them as their own. We placed them under the royal crown, and his Catholic Majesty should understand that we found these kingdoms in such order, and the said Incas governed them in such wise that throughout them there was not a thief, nor a vicious man, nor an adulteress, nor was a bad woman admitted among them, nor were there immoral people. The men had honest and useful occupations. The lands, forests, mines, pastures, houses, and all kinds of products were regulated and distributed in such sort that each one knew his property without any other person seizing or occupying it, nor were there law suits respecting it. The operations of war, though they were numerous, never interfered with the interests of commerce nor with agriculture. All things from the greatest to the most minute had their proper place and order. The Incas were feared, obeyed and respected by their subjects, as men very capable and well versed in the art of government. As in these rulers we found the power and command as well as the resistance, we subjugated them for the service of God our Lord, took away their land, and placed it under the royal crown, and it was necessary to deprive them entirely of power and command, for we had seized their goods by force of arms. By the intervention of our Lord it was possible for us to subdue these kingdoms containing such a multitude of people and such riches, and of their lords we made our servants and subjects.

'As is seen, and as I wish your Majesty to understand, the motive which obliges me to make this statement is the discharge of my conscience, as I find myself guilty. For we have destroyed by our evil example, the people who had such a government as was enjoyed by these natives. They were so free from the committal of crimes or excesses, as well men as women, that the Indian who had 100,000 *pesos* worth of gold and silver in his house, left it open merely placing a small stick across the door, as a sign that its master was out. With that, according to their custom, no one could enter nor take anything that was there. When they saw that we put locks and keys on our doors, they supposed that it was from fear of them, that they might not kill us, but not because they believed that any one would steal the property of another. So that when they found that we had thieves amongst us, and men who sought to make their daughters commit sin, they despised us. But now they have come to such a pass, in offence of God, owing to the bad example that we have set them in all things, that these natives from doing no evil, have changed into people who now do no good or very little.

'This needs a remedy, and it touches your Majesty for the discharge of your conscience, and I inform you, being unable to do more, I pray to God to pardon me, for I am moved to say this, seeing that I am the last to die of all the conquerors and discoverers, as is well known. Now there is no one but myself in this kingdom or out of it, and with this I do what I can to discharge my conscience.

'I had a figure of the sun made of gold, placed by the Incas in the House of the Sun at Cuzco, which is now the convent of San Domingo. I believe it was worth 2000 pesos, and with what I got at Caxamarca and in Cuzco, my share was worth 12,000 *pesos*. Yet I die poor and with many children. I beseech your Majesty to have pity on them, and God to have pity on my soul.'

CPSIA information can be obtained
at www.ICGtesting.com
Printed in the USA
LVHW081114230922
729105LV00011B/785